Abbot of E. Ælfric, Ebenezer Thomson

Select Monuments

of the doctrine and worship of the Catholic Church in England before the Norman conquest - consisting of Ælfric's Paschal homily and extracts from his epistles, etc.

Abbot of E. Ælfric, Ebenezer Thomson

Select Monuments

of the doctrine and worship of the Catholic Church in England before the Norman conquest - consisting of Ælfric's Paschal homily and extracts from his epistles, etc.

ISBN/EAN: 9783337286330

Printed in Europe, USA, Canada, Australia, Japan

Cover: Foto ©Lupo / pixelio.de

More available books at **www.hansebooks.com**

Godcunde Láp ꜱ Þeópdóm.

SELECT MONUMENTS

OF THE

DOCTRINE AND WORSHIP

OF THE

CATHOLIC CHURCH IN ENGLAND

BEFORE THE NORMAN CONQUEST.

CONSISTING OF

ÆLFRIC'S PASCHAL HOMILY AND EXTRACTS
FROM HIS EPISTLES, &c.,
THE OFFICES OF THE CANONICAL HOURS,
AND THREE METRICAL PRAYERS OR HYMNS.

IN ANGLO-SAXON AND PARTLY IN LATIN.

WITH

ENGLISH TRANSLATIONS
REVISED OR NEWLY EXECUTED;
NOTES, COLLATION OF ANCIENT MANUSCRIPTS,
AND
AN INTRODUCTION.

By E. THOMSON, Esq.

Second Edition.

LONDON:
JOHN RUSSELL SMITH,
36, SOHO SQUARE.
1875.

INTRODUCTION.

THE Sermon of the Paschall Lambe, the first book known to have been printed in the Saxon character, was published under the direction of Matthew Parker, Archbishop of Canterbury, and special care of his chaplain, John Joscelyn. The object of the publication was to show that the doctrine then established was not an innovation, but a revival of the doctrine maintained by the Catholic church in England before the time of the Norman Conquest.

The original publication, " Imprinted at London by Iohn Day, dwelling ouer Aldersgate beneath S. Martyns," is without date; but appears to have twice issued from the press between 1566 and

1570; as the former year contains the latest preferment, the latter the earliest removal of the prelates whose names are subscribed to a Certificate in favour of the work. A copy preserved in the British Museum evidently belongs to a second edition, as it numbers the folios from the beginning of the book, which in the copy used for this Edition commence with the Homily; it also corrects a few typographical errors of the first, as ꝑuce for ꝑice, ʒıʒ for ʒıꝑ, (see our p. 53, l. 19, and 58, 8,) as well as a misnomer in one of the Bishops, Iohn for Thomas, of Lichfield and Coventry, and divides the list differently between the two pages of the folio. And at the end, the table of ancient and modern letters is followed by a paragraph explaining the punctuation; and a separate leaf contains the colophon, a repetition of the Imprint in black letter. These minute particulars, if not formerly noticed, may be acceptable to collectors of scarce and valuable books.

The Rev. Henry Soames quotes Joscelyn's translation as if it were the work of L'Isle, and makes some corrections, which evince a knowledge of the original. But it is of more importance to observe, that the use which he has made of the Homily both in the "Bampton Lecture" and in "The Anglo-Saxon Church," proves that this "Testimony of Antiquity," which was judged to be wholesome and seasonable food for the reformed Church of England in her early years, is not contra-indicated by the symptoms of her present condition.

The Homily was republished by Foxe in his Martyrology, 2nd Edition, 1570, with some corrections in the translation; by L'Isle, along with Ælfric's Treatise on the Old and New Testament, without any of the corrections, in 1623. The translation, as amended by Foxe, was published at Aberdeen, without the original, in 1624, by Mr. William Guild, Minister at King Edward. Not having previously collated Foxe's edition, I have, in the Notes, given Mr. Guild credit for the improvements. This does not apply to the Note to p. 19, l. 5. The interpolation is not in Foxe. The old translation is also printed as an Appendix to the English of Ratramnus, Oxford, 1838.

The Extracts appended to the Homily identify the author, and leave no trace of that ambiguity which has puzzled most writers upon Ælfric during the course of three centuries. Wulfstan was Archbishop of York from 1002 to 1023: Ælfric the elder, to whom these writings are even now inconsiderately ascribed, was Archbishop of Canterbury from 995 to 1005, and, for several years before, had been a bishop and previously an abbot. To suppose the Primate of all England, near the close of a long and active public life, receiving and humbly obeying the commands of his junior, the Primate of England, to retire into a monastic cell or private study, and translate into English a voluminous treatise, which, by command of the same younger brother, he had previously drawn up in Latin, is to invert the established order of everything human and divine. Wulfstan's friend and successor was then Abbot of Peterborough, according to the ingenious Dissector of the Saxon Chronicle; but when he wrote the epistle to Wulfsine he was an humble monk or friar ("humilis frater" in both MSS.—not "presbyter" in John Retchford's transcript, as the author of the "Regular Dissection" has incautiously affirmed). This promotion was the consequence of the elder Ælfric's demise,—his successor Elphegus (Ælfheah) being translated from Winton, and the vacant See bestowed on Kenulf, Abbot of Burgh, *i.e.* Burgi [S^{ti} Petri]. The posthumous clashing of their names had no parallel collision in the contemporary tenor of their lives: the one emerges from the monastic cell when the other has retired from the archiepiscopal palace. Our author's preferment to the see of York in 1023, and his decease in 1051, are recorded in the Saxon Chronicle.

To the matter contained in Joscelyn's compilation I have added three small pieces which I had transferred to my scrap-book at different times, and which appeared suitable to the nature of the publication. The first, concerning Peter, was copied in the country some years ago from an early number of the Ælfric Society's Edition, without the translation, and under no apprehension of a disputed reading in the text. When I came to write out a copy for the press,

I persuaded myself that I must have written by mistake " ne bytlað of," where the last word should have been "ofer." An inspection of the printed text convinced me of no mistake, but did not satisfy me with regard to the reading. A MS. in the King's Library, British Museum, to which Mr. Thorpe's Preface directed me, solved all my doubts. The true reading, as I firmly believe it to be, is also, as I have since discovered, to be seen in Wheloc's Notes to Alfred's Bede, p. 238, from a MS. in the Public Library, Cambridge. His translation— Qui citra hoc fundamentum extruit—is so far good,—fabrica *sua* in ruinam magnam *assurgit*—not good.

Being haunted by no pedantic horror of pedantry, I have ventured to revive an old word here and there. The plural possessive "aller," of all, (as your, of you,) survived the parent language for many centuries. How pat, how effect ive the use of this, as of many obsolete forms, is found to be in translating from the Latin, may be shown by a single instance: 'Noster omnium hostis,' 'ure ealra feond,' 'the enemy of us all,' Chaucer would call our 'aller' (or alder) foe; thus, in "The A. B. C.,"

> And for your bothis peine, I you pray,
> Let not our alder foe make his bostaunce.

In Latin this would be, Pro vestro utriusque dolore, &c.

Ælfric's rendering of "Simon bar iona," as well as the germ of his whole exposition, is truly derived from the brief Comment of Beda on the passage. Even the name Stænen is a legitimate corollary from the words of The Venerable,—Fideli confessori sui nominis participium donavit: To the faithful confessor he gave a participation of his name. Our author, who was a good grammarian, knew how to represent the nominis participium, by converting the noun, Stan, *Rock*, into a participial form, Stænen, *Rocken*. Wheloc suggests Petræus as the corresponding Latin: Petrinus would better represent the participial form, as seen in *plenus* from the obsolete *pleo*, *egenus* from *egeo*, &c.

No writings of Wulfsine, Bishop of Sherburn, 981–998, are known to be extant; but the MS. remains of Wulfstan (Lupus) are voluminous. The specimen given, p. 102, consists of the Incipit and Explicit from one MS. and an intermediate paragraph from another MS. of the same homily. To this might be added most of the Laws of Cnut, which were very probably drawn up by this prelate. In corroboration of this view we have the Law, which Joscelyn printed according to the erroneous text of Nero, A. i., engrossed in a homily De Fide Catholica, Wheloc's Bede, p. 486, exactly as it stands, p. 80 of this Edition, the sheet being printed off before the passage was observed in Wheloc, or "The Laws and Institutes of England," edited by Mr. Thorpe, were known to be accessible. In the original edition the clause, "and hold earnestly right christendome," is omitted; but supplied by L'Isle,—one of his few improvements.

Wulfstan appears to have been a man of talent, and of a liberal and enlightened mind. On every occasion he inculcates the necessity of christian instruction, as the foundation of true piety and sound morality; that every man might learn the articles of his belief, and utter the devotions of his heart, in the language with which he was best acquainted. His "English" version of the Pater noster and Credo may be read in Wanley's Catalogue, p. 51.

To the erroneous account of our author's life and dignities, repeated in different places throughout the volume, it was not judged necessary to oppose any other argument than these few chronological notices*.

The Homily and Extracts exhibited in the first part of the volume have been esteemed clear proofs of the doctrines maintained by the catholic church of England in the tenth century, upon many points which came into controversy in later ages. The specimen of the ancient devotional forms contained in the second part, bears equal testimony to the comparative purity of worship in those early times. In the Offices we find no Ave Maria, no prayer or praise addressed to angel or saint or "maiden-mother;" of any intercessor beside the One Mediator, only a single hint.

But the most interesting feature of

---

* See also Thorpe's Preface to the Homilies, Soames, Wharton, and the Regular Dissection of the Saxon Chronicle (Hatchard, 1830).

the composition is the intermixture of the vernacular with the Latin tongue. Not only the directions, and urgent reasons for the observance of the respective Hours are given in the English of that age; but the portions of the Psalms, the Gloria, the Pater noster, and the Credo, are accompanied with a metrical paraphrase in the alliterative style and stanza of Anglo-Saxon poetry. And it is a fact worthy of notice, though not perhaps hitherto observed, that this paraphrase coincides, word for word, with the Parisian or Berry MS. edited by Mr. Thorpe, in all the portions taken from the latter half of the Psalter,—the part versified in that MS. Mr. Thorpe's publication has afforded just one correction, "lungre," ps. 59, our p. 166, for "luge" of the Worcester book, and one various reading, "eað-bede," ps. 90, for "eað-bene," p. 189. Now as these are so identified, and the quotations from the former half are also versified, may we hazard the conjecture that the framer of our Liturgy was the author of the paraphrase? The former may be the work of Ælfric, for it constitutes a part of the great compilation in which the Canons and oft-mentioned Epistles of Ælfric are included; and his talent for versification is undoubted: it is seen, or rather heard, bursting through the tissue of his prose in every part of his writings, where the subject inspires pathos or elevation of style. Even our Homily closes in alliterative strains; though we have not arranged or pointed it otherwise than the sense required in plain prose. But how probable soever this conjecture may be, neither does our author's name need any doubtful addition to its celebrity, nor is the age so barren in names that any production should remain anonymous, did history only supply the means of assigning to each his own.

Wulfstan, if we mistake not, has some pretension to poetic talent: and if Kenulf, promoted from the abbacy of Burgh to the see of Winton in 1006, was, as Mr. Kemble supposes*, the poet whose name is adumbrated by Runic characters in the Exeter Book [of Poetry] and in the Vercelli MS., we have a contemporary bard, and most probably an intimate friend and the immediate predecessor of Ælfric, with abilities equal to the highest efforts employed in adapting the Songs of Zion to Saxon measures,—the Psalms of David to the harp of Alfred.

The verses of Kenulf (Kynewulf,

---

* In the Archæologia, vols. xxviii. xxix. xxx., Papers on the Anglo-Saxon Runes, Ruthwell Cross, &c.—Mr. Kemble's Essays have resulted in one of the most glorious achievements of philological science which the present age has witnessed.—The Vercelli MS. contains the Saxon version of the Anglian staves inscribed upon the stone-pillar, "A Dream of the Cross."

ınnʀeꞃıꞃen þeaꞃꞇon heoꞃenum. ꞅy
þınnama ꞡehalꞡoꝺ cumeþınꞃıce. ꞅyþın
ꝡılla on eoꞃðan ꞅƿaꞅƿa on heoꞃenum;
ꞅyl uꞅ ꞇoꝺæꞡ uꞃneꝺæꞡhƿomlıcan
hlaꝼ. Anꝺꝼoꞃꞡyꞃ uꞅ uꞃeꞡyloaꞅ ꞅƿaꞅƿa ƿe
ꞃoꞃꞡyꝼaꝺ þuꞃum ꞡyloenꝺum. Ꞇne læꞇ þu
naþıꞃ oncoꞅꞇnunꡃe. acalyꞅ uꞅ ꝼꞃamyꝼele

(Brit. Mus. Bibl. reg. 7. C. XII fol 87a.)

Runes), to which we refer, breathe a pensive melancholy, for which we have no means of accounting from any record of his life. The Bishop of Winton (Winchester) died within a year after his promotion to that dignity.

In the Preface to the original edition, the bearing of the Homily and the other documents upon the theological discussions of that age, is distinctly stated by the writer, whether Parker or Joscelyn. In the marginal notes, too, a word of caution is affixed to some doubtful or suspected passages. These notes are all retained, only placed at the bottom of the page. The justly reprobated assertion that "The holy masse is profitable both to the lyving and to the dead," may be truly but perhaps too finely interpreted: The faithful celebration of the Lord's Supper is profitable both to the living partakers and to the same when they are dead. One passage is supposed to be interpolated or "infarced," p. 27. But it was the fashion for the preacher to entertain his audience, and enforce his argument, with a bit of legendary lore. The samples introduced here, though connected with the subject, are inconsistent with the whole tenor of the discourse. In the first fable, a child dismembered! "Is Christ divided?" Is the risen and exalted Lord, the future Judge of the world, a child? In the second, a child's finger-lith! What doubting woman, or believing man either, could be satisfied or profited by that as a substitute for a whole Saviour, the Man Christ Jesus, mature in wisdom and stature, the Son of the Living God, having power to lay down his life, and to take it up again? Could such power be conceded to a child? But to some professed believers He is always a child,—a child not emancipated from a mother's control, still worshiped as a child, and that most childishly. It is obvious, however, that the modern Romanists can make no handle of these pretended manifestations; for the child and the blood were turned to bread and wine before participation. So the Apostle Paul calls it, after the blessing or consecration (for it was not broken before that), " The Bread which we break." Neither could our author intend, by a literal interpretation of the finger-lith, to contradict his own assertion—that " It is in each man whole."

He must have regarded the matter as a temporary supersedence of the bodily sense by a supernatural manifestation of the spiritual import of the material objects presented to the eye.

For the truth of the narration Ælfric is not responsible. He gives it as he found it in The Lives of the Fathers. In fact there is nothing original in the whole of the Discourse. The literal as well as the allegorical exposition of everything recorded by Moses concerning the Passover, is substantially found in Bede's Commentary: the application of the subject to the great festival of the Christian church, and the entire argument concerning the nature of that institution, are either literally translated or liberally paraphrased from the Latin of Ratramnus.

This author was a contemporary of Paschasius, the first propounder, and apparently the original deviser of the fanciful or poetical interpretation of our Saviour's words, which was adopted by some pedants of the ecclesiastical court, and by their influence forced upon the consciences of the christian community*.

* Two centuries later, poor Berengarius was hunted down by a rival schoolmaster, Lanfranc, the future Archbishop of Canterbury, whose influence, directly or indirectly exerted to suppress

The author expresses his apprehension of its being taken for a poetic fiction, in a letter to his friend Placidus. The "bane and antidote" were produced about the middle of the ninth century.

For further information respecting these authors the reader is referred to the Bampton Lecture of Mr. Soames, and to the following publication, " Bertram or Ratram concerning the Body and Blood of the Lord, &c. Second edition, &c. London, 1688." Rabanus* Maurus, archbishop of Mentz, had written upon the same subject several years earlier, in the time of Charlemagne or his immediate successor. In a word,

the opinions, writings, and very name of our homilist, is, with great probability, supposed to have produced that obscurity which has so long brooded over Ælfric's personal identity. See the Regular Dissection, *passim*; also Ratramnus, 1688, Dissertation prefixed.

* Properly Hrabanus; so the Old German hraban, now rabe; A.-S. hræfn, now raven.

the pure Apostolic doctrine which Ratramn, with great clearness and eloquence, demonstrates from the sacred writings, and from Hieronymus, Ambrosius, Augustinus, Isidorus, &c., was not left without a witness in any age. Can we suppose that the learned men, whose opinions have been put on record, were the only persons who entertained similar opinions? Or who can ascertain the time in which some "seven thousand" true worshipers might not be found within the bounds of Christendom? The edition of "Ratram," 1688, though very inaccurately printed, is a work of merit, and might be found worthy of a corrected reprint at the present day.

The Certificate, which follows the Latin extract from the epistle to Wulfstan in the original edition, is placed immediately before the Sermon, as in L'Isle's publication.

The first thirty-six pages of this edition, Saxon and English, were in type before the editor had any charge or even knowledge of the undertaking. He had read more than once or twice the homily and translation as given by L'Isle, and had marked many things in both which required correction. This was rather a difficult task at that stage, as both the publisher and I were anxious to avoid, as far as possible, whatever might tend to enhance the price of the book. Such improvements as could be made by contrivance and economy of space were introduced; such as would have greatly disturbed the pages or paragraphs, reserved for a few notes. The Ælfric Society had not advanced so far as to include our homily, when the text was to be determined. Having only a short time before arrived in London, I had to learn what resources were at hand, and soon found in the British Museum some materials to work upon. The text, as printed by Wheloc in the Notes to Alfred's Bede, furnished some good readings, and further aid was obtained from a MS. Cott. Faustina A. IX., which, it was interesting to discover, had been collated—not for Parker's edition—but with it, and with both impressions of it; for the twofold numbering of the folios is regularly marked on the margin of the MS., and the catch-words underlined. To this MS. we owe the reading geþeode, p. 9, for gereorde, which has just occurred in a different sense, p. 2, and occurs again in the sense here intended; but another reason for the preference is the importance attached to this use of geþeode by Grimm, in relation to the name Deutsch*. It occurs in other homilies of Ælfric also, in the same sense.

* Deutsche Grammatik, 3rd ed. Einleitung.

In presenting an antidote to the ignorant corruption of Judges ix. 53, as well as to the half-learned correction in some late editions, " all-to brake," I had been anticipated by our learned printer Mr. Richard Taylor, in Notes to Boucher's Glossary. See under ALL-TO, and note to our page 27. Since going to press I have had the pleasure of seeing the same explanation in an excellent little work, Se Gefylsta, by the Rev. W. Barnes. All the old editions, those of Oxford, Cambridge, and of the British and Foreign Bible Society, retain the original reading of the translators—" all to brake;" those of Edinburgh,—Brown's, and Scott's, with Commentaries—" all to break,"—most erroneously.

The Offices were copied, without the translation, from Hickes' edition of 1705*, and afterwards collated with the

* Letters which passed between Dr. Hickes and a Popish priest, &c. Appendix. (Translation by Mr. Elstob, as the Doctor informs us.)

transcript of the famous "Book of Worcester," made by Edmund Gibson, afterwards Bishop of London, MSS. Harl. 441. (The Book of Exeter, by J. Retchford, is ibid. 438.) Gibson's transcript, executed for Dr. Hickes in 1688, coincides so exactly with the extracts printed in the little book 120 years before, that we may rely upon its accuracy as implicitly as upon the [now] Bodleian Codex Jun. 121, which was in Parker's possession at the time of printing. They agree to a letter even in the readings which I consider erroneous, and have corrected from the Book of Exeter (H. 438), or by obvious conjecture. In the Offices also some manifest errors have been corrected, as ʀynnum, p. 177; sanat, MS. for replet, p. 173, l. 6—the scribe having cast his eye upon the preceding paragraph.

In the arrangement of the metrical portion I have departed from the MS. and from the edition of Hickes and Elstob. The translation is new throughout, as literal as seemed consistent with perspicuity, and none of it *versified* (Regular Dissection, p. 194, l. 7, and 195, Note).

The three metrical prayers have been added on my recommendation. They are noticed by Hickes in his Grammar, and by Conybeare; and were by Junius characterized "genium stylumque Cædmonis probe referentes," and appended to his Cædmon; but not very accurately printed, and three whole lines omitted; so that this may be considered the first complete edition. For simplicity of style and unaffected fervour of devotion, they cannot fail to recommend themselves to every reader of the original Saxon.

To this account of the matter contained in our little volume, little needs to be added respecting the manner in which it is got up. The publisher has evinced his intention of making it a good and handsome-looking book, and the printers have taken the utmost pains to have everything as correct, neat, and well-arranged as possible. To any one who has the least experience in these matters, it will not be surprising if I should have to apologise for one or two instances of discrepancy between the plan and the execution. It was not intended to produce a *fac-simile* of the original edition as printed by J. Day, but to exhibit the text and the old translation in a correct form. Such alterations as could conveniently be made at the stage in which I became connected with the work, were introduced in their proper places; others that seemed necessary were reserved for future notice. From the number and variety of corrections, some that had been marked for insertion escaped at the time, but are taken up in the Notes.

Ꞃᵹuꞃtinuꞃ, which occurs a hundred times in MSS. as well as in printed books (see Smith's Bede, b. ii. *passim*), should have had the benefit of our Cottonian MS. as auᵹuꞃtinuꞃ.

In the Notes, G. (Guild) should have been F. (Foxe); and some abbreviations are not explained, as S. or Sax. for Saxon, A.-S. Anglo-Saxon (speech of the combined Ængle and Seaxe), Sc. Scots, acc. accusative, and a few more of no great difficulty. But, for economy of space and arrangement of the folios to suit more important matter, several illustrations from Bede, &c. were omitted. To the note on " christened" I had added—A heathen child baptized! This never was done, never can be done, by the rule and practice of any Christian church. The recipient of baptism must be a Christian—by profession if an adult, by representation (or proxy) if a child. The Philippian believed and was baptized, and in virtue of their Christian representative "all his house." The Ethiopian professed his faith in almost the very words of Peter, for he had been christened in his chariot, before Philip descended with him to the baptismal water. Bede, as translated by king Alfred, informs us that " Edwyn, king of the Northumbrians, when he was christened built a wooden church; but, after he was baptized, by the direction of bishop Paulinus built another of stone."

As christening has been ignorantly or superstitiously confounded with baptism, so another preparatory observance, " wedding," pledging or affiancing (see pages 24, 25, 2nd paragraphs), has usurped the place of marriage, to which it only gives a title. And there are many examples of similar abuse in our speech. What is " uproar"? Some of our best authorities employ the term in translating hneam, *clamour*, and a word nearly synonymous, cẏnm, as if it took its meaning from "roar;" which in reality is the *ablaut*-form of "rear," but now restricted to a secondary sense, raised or elevated sound. For the original, scriptural, and only rational meaning of "uproar," compare German *aufruhr* (the same word*), and the Greek noun *stasis*, translated by three different synonyms, in Mark, xiv. 2, xv. 7; Luke, xxiii. 19, and Acts, xix. 40, uprore, insurrection, sedition, uprore (Ed. Lond. 1734). In the last it was not the shouting, "Great is Diana of the Ephesians," that constituted the offence; but the assembling in a tumultuous manner without the authority of the magistrates. Any *uprising* against the government, however quietly it may be organized or conducted, is an UPROAR.

EBEN^R. THOMSON.

London, June 18, 1849.

* See GERMAN-ENGLISH ANALOGIES, p. 22, c. 1.

The Saxon Caracters or letters, that be moste straunge, be here knowen by other common Curacters set after them.

Ꞁ A	Ᵹ G ᵹ g	T ꞇ t
Ꞇ C	Ꝥ H	Ð þ TH ð ƿ th
D ð d	I ı i	Ƿ W ƿ w
Є E e	ꟽ M	⁊ & and
F ꝼ f	R ꞃ r	ꝥ þæꞇ
	S S ꞅ s	

N.B. *In Latin* ⁊ *is et, as* ⁊c. &c., *i. e. et cetera.*

One pricke signifieth an imperfect point, this figure; (which is lyke the Greeke interrogatiue) a full pointe, which in some other olde Saxon bookes, is expressed wyth three prickes, set in triangle wyse thus ∴.

𝔍𝔪𝔭𝔯𝔦𝔫𝔱𝔢𝔡, &𝔠.
Cum Priuilegio Regiæ
Maiestatis.

A TESTIMO-
nie of
ANTIQVITIE,
shewing the aunci-
ent fayth in the Church of England touching the sacrament of the body and bloude of the Lord here publikely preached, and also receaued in the Saxons tyme, aboue 600. yeares agoe.

Ieremie. 6.

Goe into the streetes, and inquyre for the olde way: and if it be the good and ryght way, then goe therin, that ye maye finde rest for your soules. But they say: we will not walke therein.

Imprinted at London by *Iohn Day, dwelling ouer Aldersgate beneath S. Martyns.*

THE PREFACE

TO

THE CHRISTIAN READER.

GREAT contention hath nowe been of longe tyme about the moste comfortable sacrament of the body & bloud of Christ our Sauiour: in the inquisition and determination wherof many be charged and condemned of heresye, and reproued as bringers vp of new doctryne, not knowen of olde in the church before Berengarius tyme, who taught in Fraunce, in the daies when William the Norman was by conqueste kyng of England, and Hildebrande otherwyse called Gregorius the seuenth, was pope of Rome: But that thou mayest knowe (good christian reader) how this is aduouched more boldly then truely, in especiall of some certayne men which be more ready to maintaine their old iudgement,

then of humilitie to submitte them selues vnto
a truth : here is set forth vnto thee a testimonye of verye auncient tyme, wherin is plainly
shewed what was the iudgement of the learned
men in thys matter, in the dayes of the Saxons
before the conquest. Fyrst thou hast here a
Sermon or homelye, for the holy day of Easter,
written in the olde Englishe or Saxon speech,
which doth of set purpose and at large, intreate
of thys doctryne, and is found among many
other Sermons in the same olde speech, made
for other festiuall dayes and sondayes of the
yeare, and vsed to be spoken orderly accordyng
to those daies vnto the people, as by the bokes
them selues it doth well appeare. And of such
Sermons be yet manye bookes to be seene, partlye remayning in priuate mens handes, and
taken out from monasteryes at their dissolution :
partlye yet reserued in the libraryes of Cathedrall churches, as of Worceter, Hereford, and
Exeter. From which places diuerse of these
bookes haue bene deliuered into the handes of
the moste reuerend father, Matthewe Archbyshop of Canterburye, by whose diligent search
for such writings of historye, and other monu-
mentes of antiquitie, as might reueale vnto vs
what hath ben the state of our church in Eng-

land from tyme to tyme, these thynges that bee here made knowen vnto thee, do come to lyght. Howbeit these Sermons were not first written in the olde Saxon tounge: but were translated into it, as it shoulde appeare, from the Lattyne. For about the end of a Saxon boke of lx. Sermons, (which hath aboute the middest of it this Sermon agaynst the bodely presence) be added these wordes of the translatour.

Fela ꞅæᵹeꞃe ᵹoꝺꞅpell ꝼe ꞅoꞃlæcaꝼ on ꝼꞅum bihce. Ða mæᵹ apenꝺan ꞅe ðe ꝼile; Ne ꝺuꝼꝼe ꝼe ðaꞅ boc na micle ꞅmꝼoꞃ ᵹelænᵹan. Ðꝩleꞅ ðe heo unᵹemeceᵹoꝺ ꞅꝩ. ⁊ mannum æꝼꞅæc ðuꝼh hiꞅe micelnꝩꞅꞅe aꞅciꝼuᵹe ;

We let passe many good gospells, which he that lyste may translate. For we dare not enlarge thys boke much further, lest it be ouer great, & so cause to men lothsomnes through hys bygnes. And in an other booke contaynyng some of these Saxon Sermons it is also thus written in Lattyne. In hoc codicillo continentur duodecim sermones anglice quos accepimus de libris quos Ælfricus abbas Anglice transtulit. In thys booke be comprysed xij. Sermons whiche we haue taken out of the bookes that Ælfricke abbot translated into Englishe. In which wordes truelye here is also declared who was the translatour, to witte, one Ælfricke. And so hee doth confesse of hym self in the preface of his Saxon grammer, where he doth moreouer geue vs to vnderstand the number of the Sermons that he translated thus.

Ic Ælfric wolðe ðas litlan boc awendan to englicum gereorðe of ðam stæf-cræfte ðe is gehaten grammatica. syþþan ic twa bec awende on hund eahtatigum spellum;

I Ælfricke was desirous to turne into our Englishe tounge from the arte of letters called grammer thys little booke, after that I had translated the two bookes in fourescore Sermons. But how soeuer it be nowe manifest enoughe by thys aboue declared, how that these Sermons were translated: I thinke notwithstanding, that there will hardlye be found of them any Lattyne bookes, being (I feare me) vtterlye peryshed & made out of the waye since the conquest by some which coulde not well broke thys doctrine. And that such hath bene the dealing of some partiall readers, may partlye hereof appeare. There is yet a very auncient boke of Cannons of Worceter librarye, and is for the most parte all in Lattyne, but yet intermyngled in certayne places, euen thre or foure leaues together with the olde Saxon tounge: and one place of this booke handleth thys matter of the sacrament: but a fewe lynes, wherin dyd consiste the chiefe poynt of the controuersie, be raced out by some reader: yet consider how the corruption of hym, whosoeuer he was, is bewrayed. Thys part of the Lattyne booke was taken out of ij. epistles of Ælfricke before named, & were written of hym aswell in the Saxon tounge, as the Lattyne. The Saxon epistles be yet wholie to be had in the librarye of the same church, written all in Saxon, and is intituled, a boke of Cannons, and shrift booke. But in the Church of Exeter, these epistles be seene both in the Saxon tounge, and also in the Lattyne. By the which it shall be easie for any to restore agayne, not onely the sense of the place raced in Worceter booke, but also the very same Lattyn wordes. And the words of these two epistles, so much as concerne the sacramentall bread & wyne, we here set immediatlye after the Sermon: fyrst in Saxon, then the words of the second epistle we set also in Lattyne: deliuering them most faythfully as they are to be seene in the bookes from whence they are taken. And as touching the Saxon writings, they be set out in such forme of letters, and darke speech, as was vsed, when they were written: translated also for our better vnderstanding, into our common and vsuall Englishe speech. But nowe it remayneth we do make knowen who thys Ælfricke was, whom we here speake of, in what age he liued, and in what estimation. He was truely brought vp in the scholes of Æthelwolde byshop of Winchester, Æthelwolde I meane the elder, and greate saincte of Winchester church: So canonised because in the dayes of Edgar kyng of England, he conspyred with Dunstane Archbyshop of Canterburie, & Oswalde bishop of Worceter, to expell out of the Cathedrall churches, through out all England, the maryed priestes, which then were in those churches the olde dwellers, as wryteth Ranulphus Cestrencis in hys pollicronicon, and to set vp of newe the religion or rather superstition & hipocrisie of monkes, after that the same had been a longe tyme, by the iuste iudgement of God, vtterlye abolished, the Danes spoyling them, & cruelly burning them vp in there houses, as is at large, and plentifullye confessed in the historyes of their owne churches. For thys newe rearing vp of monkerie is Æthelwolde called in moste olde historyes, pater monachorum, the father of monkes. Vnder thys Æthelwolde was Ælfricke traded vp in learning, as he witnesseth of him selfe in the Lattyne preface of his Saxon grammer, where speaking of hys interpretation of Lattyne wordes he wryteth thus. Scio multis modis verba posse interpretari, sed ego simplicem interpretacionem sequor, fastidium vitandi causa. Si alicui tamen displicuerit nostra interpretatio, dicat quomodo vult. Nos contenti sumus sicut didicimus in scholis venerabilis præsulis Æthelwoldi qui multos ad bonum imbuit. I know that wordes may be expounded diuers waies, but for to auoyde lothsomnes I doe followe the plaine interpretation. Which if any shall myslike, he may do as he thinketh best: but we are content to speake, as we haue learned in the scholes of the moste worthye byshop Æthelwolde, who hath bene a good instructour to many, or who hath brought vp many to good. This he wryteth of hym selfe. So vpon thys his education in the scholes of Æthelwolde he became afterward to be an earnest louer and a great setter forwarde of monkerye, and therefore no lesse busie writer and speaker agaynst the matrimonye of priestes in hys tyme. For which respecte he was afterwarde so regarded, that he was made by Oswalde byshop of Worceter (as reporteth Joan Capgraue) the first abbot of S. Albons newlye restored, & replenished with monkes, and was also made abbot of Malmesburye by kyng Edgar, (as reporteth William of Malmesburye) in the lyfe of Aldelmus. And truly he calleth him selfe abbot in diuers of his epistles, although he neuer named of what place, as in that he wryteth Egneshamensibus fratribus, de consuetudine monachorum; To the monkes of Egnesham, of the order and manner of monkes; and in this he wryteth here to Wulfstane Archbyshop of Yorke; and in an other agaynst priestes matrimonye sent to one Sygeferth, with whom was an anker abyding, which defended the mariage of pristes, affyrming it to be lawful. The epistle beginneth thus in the Saxon tonge.

Ælfric abb. ꞅpet Sigeferþ freondlice; Me iꞅ gerǣd þ ðu rædest beo me þ ic oþer tæhte on Englircen geþriten. oþer eoþer ancoꞃ æt ham mid eoþ tæhþ. ꞅoþþan ðe he ꞅputelice rægþ þ hit ꞅie aleꝼd. þ mæꞅꞅe pꞃeoꞅtaꞅ pel motan pifigen. and min gepꞃiten piþcꞃeþeþ ðyꞅen.

That is, Elfricke abbot doth send frendlye salutation to Sigeferth. It is tolde me that I teach otherwyse in my English writynges, then doth

thy anker teach, which is at home wyth thee.
For he sayth playnly that it is a lawfull thing for
a priest to marye, and my wrytynges doth speake
agaynst thys, &c. Thus aswell in hys owne
epistles, as in all other bookes of Sermons in
the Saxon tounge, that I haue sene, I finde him
alwaies called abbot, and onely so called. Howbeit, John Capgraue who gathered together into
one volume, the liues of English sainctes, writeth
in the life of Oswalde, that Ælfricke was laste
of all aduaunced to the Archbishops see of Canterburie. In alijs inquit Angliæ partibus insignes
ecclesias ob præfixam causam clericis euacuauit,
et eas viris monasticæ institutionis sublimauit:
quorum hæc nomina sunt: Ecclesia S. Albani,
S. Ætheldredæ virginis in Eli et ea quæ apud
Beamfledam constituta honorabilis habebatur.
Instituit enim in ecclesia S. Albani Ælfricum
abbatem, qui ad Archiepiscopatum Cantuariensem postea sublimatus fuit. In other partes of
Englande Oswald auoyded out of the most notable churches the clarkes, & aduaunced the
same places with men of the order of monkes,
whose names be these: S. Albons, the church of
the virgin S. Ætheldrede in Ely, and that which
is at Beamfleot reputed very famous. He dyd
appoynte abbot in S. Albons Ælfricke, who was

afterward promoted to the Archbyshopricke of Canterburye. Truely thys Ælfricke we here speake of, was equall in tyme to* Elfricke Archbyshop of Canterbury, as may certainly appeare to him that will well consider, when Wulfstane Archbishop of Yorke, and Wulfsine byshop of Scyrburne liued, vnto whom Ælfricke wryteth the Saxon epistles, from which the wordes concerning the Sacrament hereafter following be taken*. And the certaintye of thys consideration, may well be had out of William Malmesburye De Pontificibus, & out of the subscription of bishops, to the grauntes, letters patentes, and charters of Æthelrede†, who raigned king of England at this time. Howbeit whether this Ælfricke, & Ælfricke Archb. of Canterbury was but one, & the same man, I leaue it to other mens iudgement further to consider: for that writing here to Wulfstane, he nameth him selfe but abbot, & yet Ælfricke Archb. of Canterbury, was promoted to that his archb. stole vj. yeres before that Wulfstane was made Archbishop of Yorke*, as is declared most manifestly in the his-

* Who dyd put out secular priestes out of the church of Canterbury, as the storye of that house sheweth. † These charters are to be seene.
* Compare Introduction, pp. iv, v, vi.—ED.

toryes of Symeon of Durham, Roger Houeden, the historie of Rochester, Flores Hystoriarum, Thomas Stubbes in hys historie of the Archbishops of Yorke, and in all other moste auncient histories, aswell written in the olde Saxon tounge, as in Lattyne: Moreouer in many deedes and writynges of giftes, made by kyng Æthelrede, when Ælfricke subscribeth as Archbyshop of Canterburye, then in them is one Aldulphus, Wulfstanes predecessour, named Archbyshop of Yorke, and Wulfstane him self subscribeth but as an inferiour byshop. But be it, that this Ælfricke was onely abbot, and not Archbishop of Canterburye, yet this is also most true, that beside the prayse of great learning, & of being a most eloquent interpreter (for which William of Malmesburye doth greatly commend him), he was also of such credite and estimation to the lyking of that age in which he liued, that all his writinges, and chiefly these his epistles, were then thought to contayne sound doctrine: and the byshops them selues did iudge them full of ryghte good counsaile, preceptes, and rules to gouerne therby their clergie: and therefore dyd most earnestly request to haue these epistles sent vnto them, as doe well appeare by ij. shorte Lattyne epistles, set before the Saxon epistles wherof the one is sent to Wulfsine byshop of Scyrburne, the other to Wulfstane Archbyshop of Yorke. And after this also byshops of other churches amonge other cannons that they collected out of generall and perticular councells, out of the bookes of Gildas, out of the pœnitentialls of Theodorus, Archbyshop of Canterburye, out of the extractes of Egberhtus the iiij. Archbishop of Yorke from Paulinus: out of the epistles of Alcuinus teacher to Charles the great, and to conclude, out of the writinges of the fathers of the primatiue church: among other Cannons I saye, they collected together for the better orderyng of their churches, they doe place amonge them also these two epistles of Ælfricke, as is to be seene in ij. bokes of Cannons of Worceter librarye: whereof the one is all in the olde Saxon tounge, and there these epistles of Ælfricke be in the same tounge: the other is for the most parte all in Lattyne, and is intituled Admonitio spiritualis doctrinæ, where these epistles be in the Lattyne tounge, and be ioyned together for an exhortation to be made of the byshop to his clergie. There is also a like booke of Cannons of Exeter church, where these two epistles in Lattyne be

appoynted in stede of two sermons to bee
preached, Ad clericos et presbyteros, to the
clerkes and priestes; and the epistles bee also
in the same boke in the Saxon tonge. And
thys booke was geuen to Sainct Peters Church
in Exeter by Leofricke the first and most famous
bishop of that church, as in hys owne recorde
and graunt of all such landes, bokes, and other
thinges he gaue vnto the church, it is thus expressed in the Saxon tounge:

Þeɲe ſpucelaþ on ðiꞅꞅeɲe bec hpæt Leoꝼɲic
b. hæꝼþ ᵹeƀon into ꞅancti Petꞃeꞅ minꞅtꞃe
on Exanceaꞅtꞃe ðæɲ hiꞅ biꞅceop-ꞅtol iꞅ. þ
iꞅ þ he hæꝼþ ᵹeinnoð þ æɲ ᵹeutoð þæꞅ ðuꞃh
Goðeꞅ ꝼultume. ꞅc. ðonne iꞅ ꞅeo oncnap-
enniꞅ ðe he hæꝼþ ᵹoð mið ᵹecnaꝼen ꞅ ꞅanc-
tum Petꞃum into ðam halᵹan mýnꞅtꞃe on
cýnclicum maðmum. þ iꞅ þ he hæꝼþ þiðeɲ
innᵹeðon. ii. ꝼul mæꞅꞅe-bec. ꞅ ane colec-
taneum. ꞅ. ii. piꞅtel-bec. ꞅ. ii. ꝼulꞅanᵹ-bec.
ꞅ. i. nihtꞅanᵹ. ꞅ. i. að te leuaui. ꞅ. ii. pꞅal-
teꞃaꞅ. ꞅ ꞅe ðɲiððan ꞅpa man ꞅinᵹþ on ɲome.
ꞅ. ii. ýmneꞃaꞅ. ꞅ. i. ðeoɲꝥuɲð bletꞅunᵹ-boc.
ꞅ. iii. oþeꞃ. ꞅ þeoꞅ enᵹliꞅc Cꞃiꞅteꞅ boc. ꞅ. ii.
ꞅumeꞃ ꞃæðinᵹ-bec. ꞅ. i. pinteꞃ ꞃæðinᵹ-boc.

⁊ ꞅeᵹula canonıcoꞃum. ⁊ maꞃtyꞃoloᵹıum. ⁊.1.canon on leꝺen ⁊ ꞅcꞃıꝼt-boc on enᵹlıꞅc. &c.

Here is shewed in thys booke or charter, what Leofricke bishop hath geuen into Saint Peters mynster at Exeter, where his bishops seate is, that is, that he hath gotte in agayne through Gods helpe, what soeuer was taken out: and so forth, first shewing what landes of such as was taken from the church he recouered agayne, partlye by his earnest complaynte, and sute made for the same, partlye by his geuyng of rewardes. Nexte making also report what landes with other treasure of his owne he gaue of newe to the place: he commeth at laste to the rehearsall of hys bookes, whereof the last here named a

Canon on Leꝺen ⁊ ꞅcꞃıꝼt-boc on Enᵹlıꞅc.

that is, a Cannon boke in Lattyne, and shryfte boke in Englishe, is the boke we speake of, and hath in it the Lattyne and Saxon epistles of Ælfricke. Thus as this boke of Exeter church hath thys good euidence by which it is shewed, that Leofrike was the geuer therof: euen so the boke of Cannons of Worceter church, written all in Saxon, hath in it most certayne testimonie that the writer therof was the publike scribe of the church whose name was Wulfgeat. For thus is it recorded therin euen with the same hande of the Scribe wherin all the booke is written:

Me scripsit pulchratus scriptor pigonnen-sis; Ora obsecro pro ipsius neuis cormi ratorem; Et qui me scripsit sempes sit fælix.

Wulfgeat the scribe of Worceter churche dyd write me. Pray I besech you for hys transgressions the Creator of the worlde. And God graunt that he be alwaies happy that writ me. The other boke of Cannons of Worceter librarye, which I haue sayd is for the more part in Lattyne, and is intituled Admonitio spiritualis doctrinæ, is written in so olde a hand, as is that of Exeter church, and seemeth to be possessed of Wulfstane, who was bishop of Worceter in the dayes of William the Conquerour. And that he shoulde be the possessor of this boke I doe thus affyrme. When in his dayes Lanfranke made first this lawe of Priests in the councell he helde at Winchester, in the yeare of our Lorde 1076. Decretum est, vt nullus canonicus vxorem haheat: sacerdotum vero in castellis, vel in vicis habitantium habentes vxores non cogantur, vt dimittant: non habentes, interdicantur, vt habeant. Et deinceps caueant episcopi, vt sacerdotes, vel diaconos non præsumant ordinare, nisi prius profiteantur vt vxores non habeant. That is, It is decreed that no chanon haue a wife. But of priestes, such as haue wiues, dwelling in castels and villages, let them not be compelled to put awaye their wiues: but suche priestes as haue no wiues, forbid them to haue. And let byshops take heede that they presume not to ordaine priestes or deacons vnlesse they doe first professe to haue no wiues. Now albeit thys and many other councels held from tyme to tyme, by the space more then of an hundreth yeares after this did litle auaile, but that the priestes did both marrye, and still kepe their wiues, because as wryteth Gerardus Archbyshop of Yorke to Anselme: Cum ad ordines aliquos inuito, dura ceruice renituntur ne in ordinando castitatem profiteantur: When I call any to orders, they resiste with a stiffe necke, that they doe not in taking order professe chastitie. Or as is reported in the Saxon storye of Peterborowe church, speaking of the councells of Anselme, of Iohn of Cremona, and of William Archbyshop of Canterburye.

Ne ꝼoꞃꞅtoð noht ealle þa boðlaceꞅ.

All these decrees auailed nothing.

Ealle heolðon heꞃe piꝼeꞅ be ðeꞅ cininᵹeꞅ leaꝼ, ꞅpa ꞅpa hi eaꞃ biðon.

They all kept their wiues still by the kinges leaue, as they did before: Yet it came to passe vpon thys decree of Lanfranke, that the forme of wordes wherin the priestes should vowe chastitie, was nowe fyrst put into some bishops* pontificall. Ego frater N. promitto Deo, omnibusque Sanctis eius castitatem corporis mei secundum canonum decreta, et secundum ordinem mihi imponendum seruare domino præsule N. præsente. And as the wordes were thus put into some pontifical in a generall speaking as the manner is: So in the beginning of thys boke we here speake of, wherin be Ælfrickes epistles, be the selfe same wordes of profession written in the same olde hand as is the rest of the boke, and addeth also there the speciall name of Wulfstane byshop (who was present at

* No such demaunde of this profession in any Englyshe pontificall before this tyme.

this councell of Lanfrancke, and vnto whom it dyd fyrst appertayne to exacte of priestes in the diocesse of Worceter this profession). The wordes be these: Ego frater N. promitto Deo omnibusque sanctis eius castitatem corporis mei secundum canonum decreta, et secundum ordinem mihi imponendum domino præsule Wulfstano præsente; I brother N. doe promyse to God and all hys sainctes chastitie of my bodye, accordyng to the decrees of Cannons, and accordyng to the order to be put vpon me before Wulfstane byshop. By this I doe affirme, that this boke dyd belong to Wulfstane byshop of Worceter, and so by him was afterward geuen to the librarye of that Church, where it now remayneth. Wherefore of this now declared: first touching the sermon spoken of in the beginning, whereof, as of many other conteyned in ij. bokes, Ælfricke was but the translator, and therfore were bokes of sermons before hys time: nexte touching the publike receauing of the epistles of Ælfricke, wherin I saye is denied the bodely presence: and also by the infarcing afterward of these epistles by byshops into their bokes of Cannons in stede of exhortations to be vsed vnto their clergye: it is not hard to know, not only so much what Ælfricks iudgement was in thys controuersie, but also, that more is, what was the common receaued doctrine herein of the whole church of England, as wel when Ælfricke hym selfe lyued, as before hys tyme, and also after his time, euen from him to the conquest. But what was the condition and state of the church, when Ælfricke him self liued? In deede to confesse the truth, it was in diuers pointes of Religion full of blindnes and ignoraunce: full of childysh seruitude to ceremonies, as it was longe before and after: and to much geuen to the loue of monkerye, which now at this tyme vnmeasurablye tooke roote, and grewe excessiuely. But yet to speake what the aduersaryes of the truth haue iudged of thys time, it is most certayne, that there is no age of the church of England, which they haue more reuerenced, and thought more holy than thys. For of what age haue they canonized vnto vs more sainctes and to their lyking more notable? First, Odo Archbyshop of Canterburye, who dyed in the beginning of king Edgars reigne. Then king Edgar hym selfe, by whom Ælfricke was made abbot of Malmesburye. Then Edward called the Martyr, kyng Edgars bastard sonne. Then Editha kyng Edgars bastarde daughter. Also Dunstane archbyshop of Canterbury, of whom Ælfricke was greatly estemed. Æthelwold byshop of Winchester, vnder whom Ælfricke had his first bringing vp. Oswald byshop of Worceter, and after Archbyshop of Yorke, who made Ælfricke abbot of S. Albons. Wulfsine bishop of Scyrburne, vnto whom Ælfricke wryteth the first of the epistles we here speake of. Elfleda a nunne of Romesey, and Wulhilda Abbesse of Barkyng, lyued in the dayes of king Edgar. And laste of all Wlfritha K. Edgars concubyne. All these I say with some other more, be canonized for sainctes of this age in which Ælfricke him selfe liued in great fame and credite. Also Leofricke and Wulfsine [? Wulfstane], whom we haue shewed to haue been the geuers of those Cannon bookes wherin be seene Ælfrickes epistles, be reuerenced for moste holy men and saintes of their churches. And these ij. liued byshops in the comming in of the Conquerour. Thus doe some men now a dayes not onely dissent in doctrine from their owne church, but also from that age of their churche whiche they haue thought moste holy, and iudged a most excellent patterne to be folowed. Wherfore what may we nowe thinke of that great consent, wherof the Romanistes haue long made vaunte? to witte, their doctrine to haue continued many hundred yeares as it were lincked together with a continuall chaine, whereof hath beene no breche at any time. Truely this their so great affirmation hath vttered vnto vs no truth, as good christian reader, thou mayest well iudge by dulye weighing of this which hath beene spoken, and by the reading also of that which here followeth wherunto I now leaue thee. Trusting that after thou hast well weighed this matter of such manner of the being of Christes body in the sacrament, as sheweth this testimonye, no vntruth or dishonor shall neede to be attributed to Christes louing wordes pronounced at his laste supper among his apostles: no derogation to his most sacred institution: no diminishing of any comfort to christen mens soules in the vse of his reuerend sacrament: but all thinges to stand right vp moste agreablie both to the veritie of Christes infallible wordes, and to the right nature, congruence, and efficacie of so holy a sacrament, and finallye most comfortable to the conscience of man, for his spirituall vniting and incorporation with Christes blessed body and bloud to immortalitie, and for the sure gadge of his resurrection.

AMEN.

AS the writynges of the fathers euen of the first age of the Churche bee not thought on all partes so perfect, that whatsoeuer thyng hath been of them spoken ought to be receaued without all exception (which honour trulye them selues both knewe and also haue confessed to be onely due to the most holy and tryed word of God:) So in this Sermon here published some thynges be spoken not consonant to sounde doctrine: but rather to such corruption of greate ignoraunce & superstition, as hath taken roote in the church of long time, being ouermuch cumbred with monckery. As where it speaketh of the masse to be profitable to the quicke and dead: of the mixture of water with wyne: and wheras here is also made reporte of ij. vayne miracles, which notwithstanding seeme to haue been infarced, for that they stand in their place vnaptly, and without purpose, and the matter without them, both before & after, doth hange in it selfe together most orderly: with some other suspitious wordes sounding to superstition. But all these things that be thus of some reprehension be as it wer but by the way touched: the full and whole discourse of all the former part of the Sermon, & almost of the whole Sermon is about the vnderstanding of the Sacramentall bread & wine howe it is the bodye and bloude of Christ our Sauiour, by which is reuealed & made knowen, what hath been the common taught doctrine of the church of England on this behalfe many hundreth yeares agoe, contrarye vnto the vnaduised writyng of some nowe a dayes. Nowe that thys foresayd Saxon Homely with the other testimonies before alledged, doe fullye agree to the olde auncient bookes (wherof some bee written in the olde Saxon, and some in the Lattyne) from whence they are taken: these here vnder written vpon diligent perusing, & comparing the same haue found by conference, that they are truely put forth in Print without any adding, or withdrawing any thing for the more faithfull reporting of the same, and therefore for the better credite hereof haue subscribed their names.

 Matthewe Archbyshop of Canterburye.
 Thomas Archbyshop of Yorke.
 Edmund Byshop of London.

Iames Byshop of Durham.
Robert Byshop of Winchester.
William Byshop of Chichester.
Iohn Byshop of Hereford.
Richard Byshop of Elye.
Edwine Byshop of Worceter.
Nicholas Byshop of Lincolne.
Richard Byshop of S. Dauys.
Thomas Byshop of Lichfield and Couentrye*.
Iohn Byshop of Norwiche.
Iohn Byshop of Carlyll.
Nicholas Bishop of Bangor.

With diuers other personages of honour and credite subscribing their names, the recorde wherof remaines in the handes of the moste reuerend father Matthewe Archbishop of Canterburye.

* Iohn in 1st ed., Couentrye and Lichfield in 2nd. The Bishop of London was Grindall,—translated to York in 1570,—to Canterbury in 1576.

CONTENTS.

	Page
A SERMON OF THE PASCHALL LAMBE ..	1
EXTRACT FROM EPISTLE TO WULFSINE .	58
———————— EPISTLE TO WULFSTANE	62
———————— SAME IN LATIN	74
THE LORDES PRAYER, THE CREEDE, AND THE X. COMMAUNDEMENTS	78
EXTRACT CONCERNING PETER	94
LANGUAGE AND PLACE OF PRAYER.....	102
WULFSTAN ON THE STATE AFTER DEATH	ib.
NOTES TO THE SERMON [AND EXTRACTS]	106
THE OFFICES OF THE CANONICAL HOURS	113
METRICAL PRAYERS OR HYMNS........	212
ADDITIONAL NOTES..................	226

CORRIGENDA ET MONENDA.

P. 65, *line* 14, *for* ꞅumeneꞅ acꞃiꝼicium *read* ꞅumene ꞃacꞃiꝼicium.

P. 66, *line* 17, *for* ꞇo hiꞅ bloꝺ, *J. & L'I., read* .... bloꝺe, *as in MSS.*

P. 91, *line* 21, *for* schoolemaister *read* scholemaister, *as in* 1*st ed.*—*the double vowel, introduced by L'Isle here and elsewhere, is no more necessary than in* move, prove.

P. 121, Dꞃihꞇen Goꝺ, may be equally well, or perhaps better, Dꞃihꞇen ᵹóꝺ, good Lord: so at p. 181. Compare Dꞃihꞇen leóꝼ, Dema ᵹóꝺ, p. 213.

P. 134, *line* 12, *read* frofre.

P. 176, *Note.* Formest *is to* former *exactly as* warmest *to* warmer. See Grimm, D. Gr. iii. 627, and Professor Latham's Elements, under "Comparison of Adjectives."

The omission of the Latin text of Pater Noster and Credo was designed to preserve the continuity of the Saxon paraphrase,—which in Gloria Patri is broken by the insertion of the original words.

A SERMON
OF
THE PASCHALL LAMBE,
AND OF THE
SACRAMENTALL BODY AND BLOUD
OF CHRIST OUR SAVIOUR
WRITTEN IN THE OLDE SAXON TOUNGE BEFORE
THE CONQUEST,
AND APPOYNTED IN THE REIGNE OF
THE SAXONS
TO BE SPOKEN VNTO THE PEOPLE AT EASTER
BEFORE THEY SHOULDE RECEAUE
THE COMMUNION,
AND NOW
FIRST TRANSLATED INTO OUR COMMON
ENGLISHE SPECHE.

Men ða leoꝼoꞃtan · ʒelome eopiꞃ ʒe-ꞃæd ẏmbe uꞃeꞃ hælendeꞃ æꞃiꞃte. hu he on ðiꞃum andpeaꞃdan dæʒe æꞃteꞃ hiꞃ ðꞃopunʒe mihtiʒlice oꝼ deaþe aꞃaꞃ ; Nu pille pe eop ʒeopenian ðuꞃh Godeꞃ ʒiꝼe be ðam halʒan huꞃle ðe ʒe nu to ʒan ꞃceolon · ⁊ ʒepiꞃꞃian eopeꞃ andʒẏt ẏmbe ðæꞃe ʒeꞃẏnu. æʒþeꞃ ʒe æꞃteꞃ þæꞃe ealdan ʒecẏþnẏꞃꞃe. ʒe æꞃteꞃ þæꞃe nipan. ðẏlæꞃ ðe æniʒ tpeo-nunʒe eop deꞃian mæʒe be þam liꝼlicũ ʒeꞃeoꞃde ; Se ælmihtiʒa God bebead Moẏꞃe ðam heꞃetoʒan on eʒẏpta lande. ꝥ he ꞃceolde bebeodan Iꞃꞃahela ꝼolce · ꝥ hi namon æt ælcũ heoꞃþe aneꞃ ʒeaꞃeꞃ lamb on ðæꞃe nihte ðe hi ꝼeꞃdon oꝼ

MEN beloued, it hath bene often sayd vnto you aboute our Sauiours resurrection, how he on this present day after hys suffering, mighteiy rose from death. Now will we open vnto you through Gods grace, of the holy housell, whiche ye shoulde nowe goe vnto, and instructe your vnderstandyng aboute thys mysterie, both after the olde couenaunte, and also after the newe, that no doubting may trouble you about thys liuelye foode. The almyghtie God badde Moyses his captaine in the land of Ægypt, to commaunde the people of Israell to take for euery familye a lambe of one yeare old, the night they departed out of the countrey to the land of promise, and to offer the lambe to God, and after to kill it, and to make the signe of the crosse, with the lambes bloud vpon the side postes, and the vpper poste of their dore, and afterward to eate the lambes flesh rosted, and vnleauened bread with wilde lettisse. God said vnto Moyses: Eate of the lambe nothing raw, nor sodden in water, but rosted with fire. Eate the head, the feete, and the inwardes, and let nothing of it be left vntill the morning: if any thing thereof remaine, that shall you burne with fire. Eate it in this wyse. Gyrde your loynes, and do your shoes on your fete, haue your staues in your handes, and eat it in hast. This time is the Lordes passeouer. And ther was slain on that night, in euery house throughout Pharaos raigne, the first borne child: and Gods people of Israell were deliuered from that sodeine death

þam lande to þam behatenan earðe. ⁊ sceoldon þ lamb Gode geoffrian. and syþþan sniþan. and pyncan ꝥode tacn on heora gedyrum. ⁊ oferslegum mid þæs lambes blode. etan syþþan ðæs lambes flæsc gebræd ⁊ ðeorfe hlafas mid felðlicre lactucan; God cwæþ to Moysen. ne ete ge of ðam lambe nan þing hreap. ne on wætere gesoden. ac gebræd to fyre; Etaþ þ heafod. and þa fet. ⁊ þ innewearde. ne his nan þing ne belife oþ mergen. gif þær hwæt to lafe sy. forbærneþ þ. diczaþ hit on ðas wisan; Begyrdaþ eowre lendenu. ⁊ beoþ gesceode. habbaþ eow stæf on handa. ⁊ etaþ arðlice. ðeos tid is Godes færeld; And wearþ ða on ðære nihte ofslegen on ælcum huse geond eall Pharaones rice þ frumcennede cild. ⁊ þæs þ Godes folc Israhel ahred fram ðam færlican deaþe. Durh ðæs lambes offrunge. ⁊

his blodes meapcunȝe; þa cpæþ God
to Moyṛen. healdaþ ðiṛne dæȝ on eoṛṛū
ȝemýnde. ꞇ ꞅreolṛiaþ hine mæꞃlice on
eoṛṛum cýnṛenum mid ecum biȝenc-
ȝe. ꞇ etaþ ðeoṛṛne hlaꞅ ṛýmle ṛeoꞅan
daȝaṛ æt þiṛṛe ꞅreolṛ-tide.

Æꞅteṛ þiṛṛere dæde lædde God þ
Iṛṛahela ꞅolc oꞅeṛ ða ṛeadan ṛæ. mid
dṛium ꞅotum. ꞇ adṛæncte ðæṛon Pha-
ṛao. ꞇ ealne hiṛ heṛe ṛamod. ðe heoṛa
ehton. and aṛedde ṛýððan þ Iṛṛahela
ꞅolc ꞅeoṛeṛtiȝ ȝeaṛa mid heoꞅonlicū
biȝleoꞅan. ꞇ him ꞅoṛȝeaꞅ pæteṛ oꞅ
heaṛdum ꞅtan-clude. oþ þ hi comon to
þam behatenan eþele.

Sume ðaṛ ṛace þe habbaþ ȝetṛahtnod
on oþṛe ṛtope. ṛume þe pýllaþ nu ȝe-
openian. þ ðe delimpþ to ðam halȝan
huṛle; Cṛiṛtene menn ne moton healdan nu ða ealdan æ lichamlice. ac him
ȝedaꞅenaþ þ hi cunnon hpæt heo ȝaṛt-

through the lambes offring, and his bloudes marking. Then said God vnto Moyses. Keepe this day in your remembraunce, and holde it a greate feast in your kinredes with a perpetuall obseruation, and eate vnleauened bread alwayes seuen dayes at thys feaste.

After thys deede God ledde the people of Israell ouer the redde sea, with dry feete, and drowned therin Pharao, and al his army together, that were pursuing them; and fedde afterward the Israelits fortie yeares with heauenlye foode, and gaue them water out of the hard rocke, vntil they came to the promised land.

Part of this storye we haue treated of in an other place, part we shall now declare, to witte, that which belongeth to the holy housell. Christian men may not now kepe the olde lawe bodely, but it behoueth them to know, what it ghostlye signifieth. The innocent lambe which the old Israelites did then kill, had signification after ghostly vnderstanding of Christes suffering, who vngiltie shedde his holy bloude for our redemption. Hereof sing Gods seruauntes at euery masse:

Agnus dei qui tollis peccata mundi miserere nobis.

That is in our speech, Thou lambe of God that takest away the sinnes of the world haue mercy vpon vs.

The Israelites were deliuered from that sodaine death, and from Pharaos bondage by the lambes offringe, which signified Christes suffering: through which we be deliuered from euerlasting death, and from the deuils cruel raigne, if we rightly beleue in the true redemer of the whole world Christ the Sauiour. The lambe was offered in the euening and our Sauiour suffered in the sixt age of thys world. This age

In die Sancto Pascæ.

lice tacnie; Ðæt unscæþþiʒe lamb ðe
se ealda Israhel ða offnaþ. hæfde
ʒetacnunʒe æften ʒastlicum andʒyte
Cristes ðrowunʒe. se ðe unscæþþiʒ for
ure alysednysse his haliʒe blod aʒeat;
Be ðam sinʒaþ Godes ðeowas æt ælcere
mæssan. aʒnus dei qui tollis peccata
mundi miserere nobis; Þ is on urum
ʒeþeode. ðu Godes lamb ðe ætbrettst
middan-eardes synna ʒemiltsa us.

Þæt Israhela folc wearþ ahred fram
ðam fænlican deaþe. ⁊ fram Pharaones þeowte duph ðæs lambes of-
frunʒe. ðe hæfde ʒetacnunʒe Cristes
ðrowunʒe. duph ða we sind alysede
fram ðam ecum deaþe. ⁊ þæs re-
þan deofles anwealde. ʒif we rihtlice
ʒelyfaþ on ðone soþan alysend ealles
middan-eardes hælend Crist; Þæt lamb
wæs ʒeoffrod on æfnunʒe. and ure
hælend ðrowode on ðære sixtan ylde

ðissepe populde; Seo ylð is geteald tō
æfnunge ðises āteorigendlican middan
eardes; Þi meartcodan mid ðæs lambes
blode on heora gedyrum and ouer-
slegum tau. Þ is node tacen. ꝼ purdon
spa gescilde fram ðam engle. ðe ac-
pealde þæra egiptiscra frumcenneban
cild; And pe sceolon mearcian une
forepearde heafod. ꝼ urne lichaman
mid Cristes rode tacne. Þ pe beon ahredde fnā forpyrde. ðonne pe beoþ ge-
mearcode ægþer ge on foran heafde
ge on heortan mid blode ðære drihten-
lican ðropunge; Ðæt Israhela folc æt
ðæs lambes flæsc on heora eastes-tide
ða ða hi ahredde purdon. ꝼ pe þicgaþ
nu gastlice Cristes lichaman. ꝼ his
blod drincaþ. ðonne pe mid soþum geleafan Þ halige husel ðicgaþ; Done timan hi heoldon him to eastes-tide
seofan dagas mid micclum purþmynte

of thys corruptible worlde is reckened vnto the euening. They marked with the lambes bloude vpon the doores, and the vpper postes* Tau, that is the signe of the crosse, and were so defended from the angell that killed the Ægyptians first borne children. And we† ought to marke our foreheades, and our bodyes with the token of Christes roode, that we may be also deliuered from destruction, when we shall be marked both on forehead, and also in harte with the bloud of our Lordes suffering. Those Israelites eate the lambes fleshe at their Easter time, when they were deliuered, and we receaue ghostlye, Christes bodye, and drinke his bloude, when we receaue with true beliefe the holy housell. The tyme they kepte with

* No such signe commaunded by God in that place of scripture, but it was the bloud that God dyd loke vpon. Exod. 12.

† Vnderstand thys as that of S. Paule. Ephe. 2. Christ reconciled both to God in one body through hys crosse.

them as Easter seuen dayes with great worshippe, when they were deliuered from Pharao, and went from that land. So also we Christens kepe Christes resurrection as the time of Easter these vij. dayes, because through hys suffering and rising we be deliuered, and be made cleane by going to this holy housell, as Christ sayth in his gospell: Verely, verely, I saye vnto you, ye haue no life in you except ye eate my flesh, and drinke my bloud. He that eateth my flesh, and drinketh my bloud, abideth in me, and I in him, and hath the euerlasting life, and I shall raise him vp in the laste day. I am the liuely bread, that came down from heaven, not so as your forefathers eate the heauenlye bread in the wildernesse, and afterwarde dyed. He that eateth thys bread, he liueth for euer. He blessed bread before his suffering, and deuided it to his disciples, thus saying:

In die Sancto Pascæ.

ðe hi ahnedde pundon piþ Pharao. ⁊ of ðam earde fendon. fpa pe eac cristene menn healdaþ Cristes ærist uf to easten-tide ðas geofan dagas. fonþan ðe pe sint ðuph his ðrorunge and ærist alysede. ⁊ pe beoþ geclænsode ðuph ðæs halgan hufel-ganges. fpa fpa Crist sylf cpæþ on his godspelle; Soþ soþ ic eop secge. næbbe ge lif on eop. buton ge eton min flæsc. ⁊ drincon min blod; Se ðe et min flæsc. ⁊ min blod drincþ. he punaþ on me. and ic on him. and he hæfþ þ ece lif. and ic hine aræfe on ðam endenextan dæge; Ic eom se liflica hlaf ðe of heofonum astah. na fpa fpa eopefe sonþ-fædefas æton ðone heofonlican hlaf on peftene. and fyþþan fpulton; Se ðe et ðisne hlaf. he leofaþ on ecnyffe; Þe halgode hlaf æn his þrorunge. and todælde his discipulum ðus cpeþende. Etaþ ðisne hlaf. hit is min lichoma. and doþ þis on mynum gemynde; Eft he bletsode pin on anum calice. and cwæþ; Drincaþ ealle of ðisum. ðis is min blod. þ ðe biþ for manegū agoten on synna forgyfenysse.

Ða apostoli dydon swa swa Crist het. þ hi halgodon hlaf and pin to husle eft syþþan on his gemynde; Eac swylce heora æfter-gengan. and ealle sacerdas be Cristes hæse halgiaþ hlaf ꝥ pin to husle on his naman mid þære apostolican bletsunge.

Nu smeadon gehwilce men oft. and git gelome smeagaþ. hu se hlaf ðe biþ of corne gegearcod. and ðurh fyres hætan abacen. mage beon awend to Cristes lichaman. oððe ꝥ pin þe biþ of manegum berium awrungen. weorþe awend ðurh ænigre bletsunge to Drihtnes blode; Nu secge we gehwilcum

Eate thys bread, it is my body, and do this in my remembraunce. Also he blessed wyne in a cuppe, and said: Drinke ye all of thys. This is my bloude, that is shedde for many, in forgeuenesse of sinnes.

The Apostles dyd as Christ commaunded, that is, they blessed bread and wine to housell agayne afterward in hys remembraunce. Euen so also their successoures, and all priestes, by Christes commaundement, doe blesse bread and wine to housell in hys name with the Apostolike blessing.

Now seueral men haue often* searched, and do yet often search, howe bread that is gathered of corne, and through fyers heate baked, may bee turned to Christes body, or how wyne that is pressed out of many grapes is turned through any blessing to the Lordes bloude.

* This was now in question, and so before Beringarius tyme.

Now saye we to suche men, that some thinges be spoken of Christ by * signification, some by thyng certaine. True thyng is and certaine, that Christ was borne of a maide, and suffred death of his own accorde, and was buried, and on thys daye rose from death. He is sayd bread by signification, and a lambe, and a lyon, and so forth. He is called bread, because he is our life and angells life. He is sayd to be a lambe for his innocencie. A lyon for strength, wherwith he ouercame the strong deuill. But Christ is not so notwithstanding after true nature, neither bread, nor a lambe, nor a Lyon.

Why is then the holy housel called Christs body, or his bloud, if it be not truely that it is called? Truely the bread and the wine which by the masse of the priest be halowed, shewe one thyng

---

* A necessarye distinction.

In die Sancto Pascæ.

mannum. Þ sume ðing sind gecpedene be Criste ðurh getacnunge. sume ðurh gesissum dinge; Soþ ðing is and gesis. Þ Crist pæs of mædene acenned. ꝼ sylf-pilles ðropode deaþ. and pæs bebyrized. ꝼ on ðisum dæge of deaþe aras; He is gecpeden hlaf ðurh getacnunge. and lamb. ꝼ leo. and gehu elles; He is hlaf gehaten. forþan ðe he is ure lif ꝼ engla; He is lamb gecpeden for his unscæþþignysse; Leo for ðære strencþe. ðe he oferspiðde ðone strangan deoful; Ac spa-ðeah æfter soþum gecynde. nis Crist naþor ne hlaf. ne lamb. ne leo;

Þis is ðonne Þ halige husell gecpeden Cristes lichama. oþþe his blod. gif hit nis soþlice Þ Þ hit gehaten is; Soþlice se hlaf and Þ pin ðe beoþ ðurh sacerda mæssan gehalgode oþer ðing

hi æteoþiaþ menniscum andgitum wiþutan. and oþen ðing hi clýpiaþ wiþinnan
gelearfullum modum ; wiþutan hi beoþ
geferene hlaf ꝯ win ægþer ge on hiwe ge
on swæcce. ac hi beoþ soþlice æfter
þære halgunge Cristes lichama and
his blod ðurh gastlice geryne ; Hæþen
cild bið gefullod. ac hit ne bret na his
hiw wiþutan ðeah ðe hit beo wiþinnan
awend ; Hit bið gebroht synfull ðurh
adames forgægednysse to ðam font-
fate ; Ac hit bið aþogen fram eallum
synnum wiþinnan. ðeah ðe hit wiþutan
his hiw ne awende ; Eac swylce þ halige
font-wæter. ðe is gehaten lifes wyl-
spring. is gelic on hiwe oðrū wæterum.
and is underðeod brosnunge. ac ðæs
halgan gastes miht geneoalæcþ þam
brosnigendlicum wætere ðurh sacerda
bletsunge. ꝯ hit mæg syþþan lichaman
ꝯ sawle aþwean fram eallum synnū þurh

witnout to humayne vnderstanding and an other thing they call within to beleuing mindes. Without they bee sene bread and wine both in figure and in tast: but they be truely after the halowing, Christes body and hys bloude through ghostly mistery. An heathen childe is baptized, yet he altereth not hys shape without though he be chaunged within. He is brought to the font-vat sinfull through Adams disobedience. Howbeit he is washed from all sinne within, though he hath not chaunged his shape without. *Euen so the holy fonte-water that is called the welspryng of lyfe is lyke in shape to other waters, and is subiecte to corruption, but the holy Ghostes might commeth to the corruptible water through the priestes blessing, and it may after wash the body and soule from all sinne, through ghostly myghte.

* The water in baptisme, and bread and wyne in the Lordes supper, compared.

Beholde nowe wee see two thynges in this one creature. After true nature the water is corruptible water, and after ghostlye misterye, hath healing mighte. So also if wee beholde the holye housell after bodely vnderstanding, then see we that it is a creature corruptible and mutable: if we acknowledge therein ghostly myght, than vnderstand we that lyfe is therin, and that it geueth immortalitie to them that eate it with beliefe.

Muche is betwixte the inuisible myghte of the holye housell, and the visible shape of hys proper nature. It is* naturally corruptible bread, and corruptible wine: and is by myghte of Gods worde truely Christes bodye, and hys bloude: not so notwithstanding bodely, but ghostly. Much is betwixte the †body Christ suffred in, and the

---

* No transubstantiation.

† Differences betwixt Christes naturall body, and the Sacrament therof.

ȝaſtlice mihte; Efne nu þe ȝeſeoþ þa ðinȝ on ðiſum anum ȝeſceafte; Æfteſ ſoþum ȝecẏnde þ pæteſ iſ bſoſnienðlic pæta. ꝛ æfteſ ȝaſtlicſe ȝeſẏnu hæfþ halpende mihte; Spa eac ȝif pe ſceapiaþ þ haliȝe huſel æfteſ lichamlicū anðȝite. ðonne ȝeſeo pe þ hit iſ ȝeſceaft bſoſnienðlic ꝛ apendeðlic; Gif pe ða ȝaſtlican mihte ðæſon tocnapaþ. ðonne undeſȝite pe þ ðæſ iſ liſ on. anð foſȝifþ undeaðlicnẏſſe ðam ðe hit mið ȝeleaſan þicȝaþ.

Micel iſ betpux ðæſe unȝeſepenlican mihte ðæſ halȝan huſleſ. and ðam ȝeſepenlican hipe aȝeneſ ȝecẏndeſ; Ƿit iſ on ȝecẏnde bſoſnienðlic hlaf. and bſoſnienðlic pin. ꝛ iſ æfteſ mihte ȝodcundeſ poſðeſ. ſoþlice Cſiſteſ lichama. and hiſ blod. na ſpaþeah lichamlice. ac ȝaſtlice; Micel iſ betpux ðam lichaman ðe Cſiſt on ðſopode.

and ðam lichaman ðe to huſle biþ gehalgod; Se lichama ſoþlice ðe Criſt
on ðropode pæſ gebopen oſ Marian
flæſce. mid blode ꝩ mid banum. mid
felle ꝩ mid ſinum. on menniſcū limum.
mid geſceadpiſne ſaple gelifſæſt. ꝩ hiſ
gaſtlica lichama ðe pe huſel hataþ iſ oſ
manegum coſnum gegadeſod. buton
blode ꝩ bane. limleaſ ꝩ ſapulleaſ.
and niſ ſoþþi nan ðing ðæron to
undeſſtandenne lichamlice. ac iſ eall
gaſtlice to undeſſtandenne; Spa hpæt
ſpa on ðam huſle iſ ðe uſ liſeſ edpiſt
forgiſſ. þ iſ oſ ðæne gaſtlican mihte.
and ungeſepenlicſe fremmincge; Forþi
iſ þ halige huſel gehaten geſýnu. foſi-
þan ðe oþeſ ðing iſ ðæron geſepen.
and oþeſ ðing undeſgiten; Ðæt þ ðæſ
geſepen iſ hæſþ lichamlic hip. ꝩ þ þ
pe ðæron undeſſtandaþ hæſþ gaſtlice
mihte.

bodye that is halowed to housell. The body truely that Christ suffered in was borne of the *flesh of Mary, with bloud and with bone, with skinne and with synowes, in humane limmes, with a reasonable soule liuing: and his ghostlye body, whiche we call the housell, is gathered of many cornes: without bloude and bone, without lymme and without soule: and therfore nothing is to be vnderstode therein bodelye, but all is ghostlye to be vnderstode. What soeuer is in that housell, whiche geueth substaunce of lyfe, that is of the ghostlye might, and inuisible doing. Therfore is the holy housel called a misterye, because there is one thing in it seene, and an other thing vnderstode. That which is ther †sene, hath bodely shape: and that we do there vnderstand, hath ghostlye might.

* 1. Difference. fred is in the housell.
* Not the body that suffred is in the housell.
† 2 Difference.

Certaynely Christes bodye which suffred death, and rose from death, neuer *dyeth henceforth: but is eternall and vnpassible. The housell is temporall, not eternall. †Corruptible, and dealed into sondrye partes. Chewed betwene teeth, and sent into the bellye: howbeit neuerthelesse after ghostlye myght, it is all in euery part. Manye receaue the holye body: and yet notwithstandyng, it is so all in euerye parte after ghostly mystery. Though to some man fall a lesse deale, yet is there no more myghte notwithstandyng in the more parte, then in the lesse: because it is all in each man after the inuisible myght.

Thys misterye is a ‡pledge and a figure: Christes bodye is truth itselfe. Thys pledge we doe keepe mistically, vntill that we be come to the truth itselfe: and then is this pledge ended.

* 3. Difference.   † 4. Difference.
‡ 5. Difference.

In die Sancto Pascæ.

Witodlice Cristes lichama ðe deaþ ðrorode. and of deaþe aras. ne swylt næfre heonon forþ. ac is ece and unþrowiendlic; þæt huru is hrilpendlic. na ece; Brosniendlic. ⁊ biþ sticc-mælum todæled; Betwux toþum tocowen. and into ðam buce asend. ac hit biþ ðeah hwæþere æfter gastlicre mihte on ælcum dæle eall; Maneᵹa underfoþ ðone halᵹan lichaman. and he biþ swa ðeah on ælcum dæle eall æfter gastlicre ᵹerynu; Deah sumū menn ᵹesceote læssa dæl. ne biþ swa-ðeah na mare miht on ðam maran dæle ðonne on ðam læssan. for ðan ðe hit biþ on ælcum menn ansund æfter ðære unᵹesewenlican mihte.

Þeos ᵹerynu is wedd and hiw; Cristes lichama is soþfæstnyss; Ðis wedd we healdaþ ᵹerynelice. oþ þ we becumon to ðære soþfæstnysse. and þonne biþ þis wedd ᵹeendod; Soþlice

hit is swa swa þe ær cwædon Cristes
lichama. and his blod. na lichamlice
ac gastlice; Ne sceole ge smeagan hu
hit gedon sy. ac healdan on eowrum
geleafan þ hit swa gedon sy;

Þe rædaþ on þære bec. ðe is gehaten uitas patrum. þ twegen munecas
abædon æt Gode sume swutelunge be
þā halgan husle. and æfter þære bene
gestodon him mæssan; Ða gesawon hi
licgan an cild on þam weofode ðe se
mæsse preost æt mæssode. and Godes
engel stod mid handsexe anbidiende
oþ þ se preost þ husel tobræc; Þa
tolyþode se engel þ cild on ðam disce.
and his blod into ðam calice ageat;
Eft ða ða hi to ðam husle eodon. ða
wearþ hit apend to hlafe. and to wine.
and hi hit ðygedon. Gode ðancigende
ðære swutelunge; Eac se halga Gregorius abæd æt Criste. þ he æteowede

Truelye it is so as we before haue said Christes bodye, and hys bloude: not bodelye, but ghostlye. And ye shoulde not searche how it is done, but hold it in your beliefe that it is so done.

We read in the booke which is called *vitas patrum,* that two* Monkes desired of God some demonstration touchyng the holy housell, and after as they stoode to heare masse, they sawe a childe lying on the alter, where the priest sayd masse, and Gods Aungell stoode with a sworde, and abode lookyng vntill the priest brake the housell. Then the angell deuided that childe vpon the dyshe, and shedde his bloud into the chalice. After, when they did go to the housell, then was it turned to bread and wine, and they dyd cate it geuing God thankes for the shewing. Also S. Gregory desired of Christ, that he would shew to a certain woman

* These tales seme to be infarced.

doubting about his mysterye some great affyrmation. She went to housell with doubting minde, and Gregorye forthwith obtained of God, that to them both was shewed that part of the housell which the woman should receaue, as if there lay in the dish a ioynte of a finger al bebloded: and so the womans doubting was then forthwith healed.

Let vs now heare the apostles wordes about this misterye. Paule the apostle speaketh of the old Israelites, thus writing in his epistle to faithfull men. All our forefathers were baptised in the cloud, and in the sea: and all they ate the same ghostlye meate, and dranke the same ghostly drinke. They dranke truly of the stone that followed them, and that stone was Christ. Neither was the *stone then from whiche the water

---

* Note this exposition, which is now a daye͞ thought new.

In die Sancto Pascæ. 29

anū trymzendum piɾe embe hiꞅ ʒeꞃÿnu micele ꞅeþunʒe; Ꝥeo eode to huꞅle mid trymzendum mode. ꞏj Gꞃeʒoꞃiuꞅ beʒeat æt Gode dæꞃꞃihte. Ꝥ him bam peaꞃþ æteoped ꞅeo ꞅnæd dæꞅ huꞅleꞅ. de heo dicʒan ꞅceolde. ꞅpÿlce þæꞃ læʒe on þam diꞅce aneꞅ ꞅinʒꞃeꞅ liþ eall be-blodʒod. ꞏj dæꞅ piꞅeꞅ tpeonunʒ peaꞃþ da ʒeꞃihtlæced.

Vton nu ʒehÿꞃan dæꞅ apoꞅtoleꞅ poꞃd embe daꞅ ʒeꞃÿnu; Pauluꞅ ꞅe apoꞅtol cpæþ be dam ealdan ꞅolce Iꞅꞃahel. duꞅ pꞃitende on hiꞅ piꞅtole to ʒeleaꞅꞅullū mannum; Ealle uꞃe ꞅoꞃþ-ꞅæderaꞅ pæꞃon ʒeꞅullude on polcne. and on ꞅæ. and ealle hi æton done ÿlcan ʒaꞅtlican mete. and ealle hi dꞃuncon done ÿlcan ʒaꞅtlican dꞃenc; Ꝥi dꞃuncon ꞅoþlice oꞅ æꞅteꞃꞅiliʒendan ꞅtane. ꞏj ꞅe ꞅtan pæꞅ Cꞃiꞅt; Næꞅ ꞅe ꞅtan de Ꝥ pæteꞃ þa oꞅ ꞅleop lichamlice Cꞃiꞅt. ac he ʒe-

tacnode Críſt. ðe clýpode þuſ to eallū
ᵹeleaffullū mannū. ſƿa hƿam ſƿa
ðyrſte cume to me 7 drince; And of
hiſ innoþe fleopþ lifliċ ƿæter; Þiſ he
ſæde be ðam halᵹan ᵹaſte ðe ða under-
fenᵹon. ðe on hine ᵹelýfdon.

Se apoſtol Pauluſ cƿæþ. þ þ Iſrahela
folc æte ðone ylcan ᵹaſtlican mete.
and drunce ðone ilcan ᵹaſtlican drenc.
forþan þe ſe ylca heofonlica mete ðe
hi afedde. xl. ᵹeara. 7 þ ƿæter ðe of
ðam ſtane fleop. hæfde ᵹetacnunᵹe
Criſteſ lichaman. and hiſ blodeſ. ðe
nu beoþ ᵹeoffrode dæᵹhƿolice on Godeſ
cýrcan; Þit ƿæron þa ylcan ðe ƿe nu
offriaþ. na lichamlice. ac ᵹaſtlice.

Ƿe ſædon eoƿ hƿene ær. þ Criſt
halᵹode hlaf 7 ƿin ær hiſ þroƿunᵹe to
huſle. and cƿæþ. ðiſ iſ min lichama.
and min blod; Ne ðroƿode he ða ᵹyt.

ranne bodelye Christ, but it signifyed Christ, that calleth thus to al beleauing and faithful men : Who soeuer thirsteth let him come to me and drinke. And from his boweles floweth lyuely water. This he sayd of the holy ghost, whom he receaueth which beleaueth on hym.

The apostle Paule sayth, that the Israelites did eat the same ghostly meate, and drinke the same ghostly drinke : bycause the heauenly meate that fedde them fourtye yeares, and the water which from the stone did flowe, had signification of Christes bodye, and his bloude, that nowe be offered daylye in Gods churche. It was the same which we now offer: not bodely, but ghostly.

We sayd vnto you a little before, that Christ halowed bread and wyne to housell before his suffering, and sayd: This is my body, and my bloud. Yet he had not then suffred; but so notwithstanding he* turned through inuisible might the bread to hys owne body, and the wyne to his bloode, as he before did in the wildernes, before that he was borne a man, when he† turned that heauenly meate to his fleshe, and the flowing water from the stone to hys owne bloude. Verye many ate of the‡ heauenlye meate in the wildernes, and dranke the ghostlye drinke and were neuertheles dead, as Christ sayd. And Christ ment not the death whiche none can escape: but the euerlastynge death, whiche some of the folke deserued for their vnbeliefe. Moyses and Aaron, and many other of the people whiche pleased God eate the heauenly bread, and they dyed not the euerlasting death, though they dyed the common death. They sawe

---

* Now we eate that bodye which was eaten before he was boren by the faythfull.
† See a transubstantiation.   ‡ Manna.

ac ꞅpa ðeah he apenðe ðuꞃh unᵹeꞃepen‐
lice mihte ðone hlaꝼ to hiꞅ aᵹenum
lichaman. anð ꝥ pin to hiꞅ bloðe. ꞅpa
ꞅpa he æꞃ ðyðe on ðam peꞅtene. æꞃi
ðan ðe he to men ᵹeboꞃen puꞃðe. ða
ða he apenðe ðone heoꝼonlican mete
to hiꞅ ꝼlæꞅce. anð ꝥ ꝼlopenðe pæteꞃ oꝼ
ðam ꞅtane to hiꞅ aᵹenum bloðe ; Fela
manna æton oꝼ ðam heoꝼonlican mete
on ðam peꞅtene. anð ðꞃuncon ðone
ᵹaꞅtlican ðꞃenc. anð puꞃðon ꞅpa‐ðeah
beaðe. ꞅpa ꞅpa Cꞃiꞅt ꞅæðe ; Ne mænðe
Cꞃiꞅt ðone beaþ ðe nan mann ꝼoꞃbuᵹan
ne mæᵹ. ac he mænðe ðone ecan beaþ
ðe ꞅume oꝼ ðam ꝼolce ꝼoꞃ heoꞃa ᵹe‐
leaꝼleaꞅte ᵹeeaꞃnoðon ; Moyꞅeꞅ anð
Aaꞃon. ⁊ maneᵹa oþꞃe oꝼ ðam ꝼolce
ðe Goðe ᵹelicoðon. æton ðone heoꝼon‐
lican hlaꝼ. ac hi næꞃon beaðe ðam
ecum beaþe. ðeah ðe hi ᵹemænū beaþe
ꝼoꞃþ‐ꝼeꞃðon ; Þi ᵹeꞅapon ꝥ ꞅe heoꝼon‐

In die Sancto Pascæ.

lica mete þæs ȝesepenlic. ꝛ bnosmenb-
lic. ac hi undersrodon ȝasrlice be ðam
ȝesepenlican ðinȝe. and hit ȝasrlice
ðiȝdon;

Se hælend cpæþ. se ðe et min flæsc.
ꝛ drincþ min blod. he hæfþ ece lif;
Ne het he na etan ðone lichaman. ðe
he mid befanȝen þæs. ne þ blod druncan.
ðe he fon us aȝeat. ac he mænde mid
þam posde þ haliȝe husel. ðe ȝastlice is
his lichama and his blod. and se þe þæs
onbyriȝþ mid ȝeleaffulse heostan. he
hæfþ þ ece lif;

On ðæse ealdan æ ȝeleaffulle men
offrodon Gode miʃclice lac. ðe hæfdon
toseaþde ȝetacnunȝe Cristes lichaman.
ðe sylf fon usum synnū syþþan ȝeof-
frode his heofonlican fæder to onsæ-
ȝednysse;

that the heauenlye meate was visible and corruptible; but they ghostly vnderstode by the visible thing, and ghostly receyued it.

The Sauiour sayde: He that eateth my fleshe, and drinketh my bloud, hath euerlasting lyfe. He bad them not eate the body which he was encompassed with, nor the bloud to drink which he shed for vs: *but he ment with those wordes the holy housell, which ghostly is his body, and his bloud, and he that tasteth it with beleauing hart, hath the eternall lyfe.

In the old law faithful men offred to God diuers sacrifises, that had† foresignification of Christes body, which for our sinnes he himselfe to his heauenly father hath since ‡ offred as a sacrifice.

* What body doe the faythfull now eate.
† A signification before Christ.
‡ A sacrifice in Christes tyme.

Certaynly this housell whiche we doe nowe halow at Gods alter is a* remembraunce of Christes body which he offred for vs, and of his bloude whiche he shedd for vs: So he him selfe comaunded: Do thys in my remembraunce. Once suffred Christe by hym selfe, but yet neuerthelesse hys suffrynge is daylye renued at the masse through mysterye of the holye housell. Therfore the holye masse is profitable both to the lyuing and to the dead: as it hath bene often declared.

We oughte also to consyder diligently how that the holy housell is both Christes body, and the body of all† faythfull men, after ghostly mysterye. As the wyse Augustine sayeth of it: Yf ye will vnderstand of Christes body, heare the apostle Paule thus speaking: Ye truly be Christes body and his

---

* A remembraunce after Christ.
† The housell is also the body of al faithfull men.

In die Sancto Pascæ.

Witodlice ðis husel þe nu biþ gehalgod æt Godes peofode. is gemÿnd Cristes lichaman ðe he for us geoffrode. ꝛ his blodes ðe he for us ageat. swa swa he sylf het. Doþ þis on minum gemÿnde; Æne þrorode Crist þurh hine sylfne. ac swa-þeah dæghpomlice biþ his ðrorung geednirod þurh gerÿnu ðærs halgan husles æt ðære halgan mæssan; Forði fremaþ seo halige mæsse micclum ge ðam libbendum. ge ðam forþ-farenum. swa swa hit for oft gesputelod is;

Us is eac to smeagenne. þ þ halige husel is ægþer ge Cristes lichama. ge ealles geleaffulles folces. æfter gaftlicre gerÿnu; Spa swa se wisa Agustinus be ðam cpæþ; Gif ge pillaþ understandan be Cristes lichaman. gehÿraþ þone apostol Paulum þus cpeþende Ge soþlice sindon Cristes lichama ꝛ

In die Sancto Pascæ.

leoniu; Nu iſ eopeꞃ ᵹeꞃẏnu ᵹeleð on Goðeſ mẏꞃan. anð ᵹe unðeꞃꝼoþ eopeꞃ ᵹeꞃẏnu co þam ðe ᵹe ꞃẏlꝼe ꞃinð; Beoþ ꝥ ꝥ ᵹe ᵹeꞃeoþ on þam peoꞃoðe. anð unðeꞃꝼoð ꝥ ꝥ ᵹe ꞃẏlꝼe ꞃinð; Eꝼc cpæþ ꞃe apoꞃcol Pauluꞃ be ðiꞃum. Þe manega ꞃẏnðon an hlaꝼ. ꞇ an lichama; Unðeꞃꞃcanðaþ nu anð bliꞃꞃiaþ. ꝼeala ꞃinð an hlaꝼ ꞇ an lichoma on Cꞃiꞃce; Þe iꞃ uꞃe heaꝼoð. ꞇ pe ꞃinð hiꞃ lima; Ne bið ꞃe hlaꝼ oꝼ anum coꞃne. ac oꝼ maneᵹum; Ne ꝥ pin oꝼ anꞃe beꞃian. ac oꝼ maneᵹum; Spa pe ꞃceolon eac habban annẏꞃꞃe on uꞃum Dꞃihcne. ꞃpa ꞃpa hic apꞃicen iꞃ be þam ᵹeleaꝼꝼullan peoꞃoðe. ꝥ hi pæꞃon on ꞃpa micelꞃe annẏꞃꞃe. ꞃpilce him eallum pæꞃe an ꞃapul. ꞇ an heoꞃce; Cꞃiꞃc ᵹehalᵹoðe on hiꞃ beoðe ða ᵹeꞃẏnu uꞃe ꞃibbe ꞇ uꞃe annꞃꞃꞃe. ꞃe þe unðeꞃꝼehþ ðæꞃe annẏꞃꞃe ᵹeꞃẏnu. ꞇ ne hilc þone benð ðæꞃe ꞃoþan ꞃibbe. ne unðeꞃꝼehþ he na ᵹeꞃẏnu ꝼoꞃ him

members. Nowe is your mysterye sett on Godes table; and ye receyue your mysterye to that whiche ye your selues be. Be that whiche ye se on the alter, and receiue that whiche ye your selues be. Agayn, the Apostle Paule sayth by it: We manye be one bread, and one bodye. Vnderstand nowe, and reioyce; many be one bread, and one body in Christ. He is our head, and we be his limmes. And the bread is not of one corne, but of many. Nor the wyne of one grape, but of manye. So also we all should haue one vnitie in our Lord, as it is written of the faithfull armye, how that they were in so great an vnitie, as though all of them had one soule, and one harte. Christ hallowed on hys table the mysterye of our peace, and of our vnytye: he whyche receyueth the mysterye of vnytye, and kepeth not the bonde of true peace, he receyueth not a mysterye for hym selfe, but a witnesse agaynst hym selfe.

It is very good for Christen men, that they goe often to housell, if they brynge wyth them to the alter innocencye in their harte; if they be not possessed with vices. To the euill man it turneth to no good, but to destruction, if he receiue vnworthily the holy housell.

Holy* bookes commaund that water be mengled to the wine which shal be for housell: because the water signifieth the people, and the† wine Christs bloud. And therfore shall neither the one without the other be offred at the holy masse: that Christ may be with vs, and we with Christ; the head with the lymmes, and the lymmes with the head.

We would before haue intreated of the lambe whyche the olde Israelites offered at theyr Easter-tyme, but that we de-

---

* No Scripture inforceth the mixture of water with the wyne.

† The wine signifieth Christes bloude.

In die Sancto Pascæ.

sylfum. ac zecýðnýsse togeanes him
sylfum;

Micel ᵹód biþ cristenum mannum þ
hi ᵹelome to husle ᵹan. ᵹif hi unscæþ-
þiᵹnýsse on heora heortan beraþ to
ðam weofode. ᵹif hi ne beoþ mid leah-
trum ofsette; þam ýfelan men ne be-
cýmþ to nanum ᵹóde. ac to forwýrde.
ᵹif he ðæs halᵹan husles unwurþe on-
býriᵹþ;

Haliᵹe béc beodaðþ man ᵹemæncᵹe
wætes to ðam wine ðe to husle sceal;
forþan þe þ wæter hæfþ þæs folces ᵹetacnunᵹe. swa swa þ win Cristes blódes;
And forði ne sceal naþor buton oðrum
beon ᵹeoffrode æt ðære halᵹan mæssan. þ Crist beo mid us. ⁊ we mid
Criste. þ heafod mid ðam leomum. ⁊
þa leomu mid þam heafode;

We woldon ᵹefýrn trahtnian be þam
lambe þe se ealde Israhel æt heora

In die Sancto Pascæ.

eaſten-tẏde ʒeoffnodon · ac þe poldon æneſt eop ʒenæccan ẏmbe ðaſ ʒenẏnu · ⁊ ſẏþþan hu hit man ðicʒan ſceal; Đæt ʒetacniendlice lamb þæſ ʒeoffnod æt heoſa eaſten-tide · ⁊ ſe apoſtol Pauluſ cpæþ on ðiſum bæʒþeſlicum piſtole · þ Cſiſt iſ uſe eaſten-tid · ſe ðe fon uſ þæſ ʒeoffnod · ⁊ on ðiſum dæʒe of deaþe aſaſ;

Iſnahel ðiʒde ðæſ lambeſ flæſc · ſpa ſpa God bebead · mid ðeonſum hlafum · ⁊ feldlicum lactucum · ⁊ pe ſceolon ðicʒan þ haliʒe huſel Cſiſteſ lichaman ⁊ hiſ blod buton beoſman ẏfelnẏſſe ⁊ mánfulnẏſſe; Spa ſpa ſe beoſma aſent þa ʒeſceaſta of heoſa ʒecẏnde · ſpa apendað eac leahtſaſ ðæſ manneſ ʒecẏnde fſam unſceaþþiʒnẏſſe to ʒepemmednẏſſe; Se apoſtol tæhte þ þe ſceoldon ʒepiſtfullian na on ẏfelnẏſſe beoſman · ac on ðeonfnẏſſum ſifeſnẏſſe

sired first to declare vnto you of this mysterye, and after how we should receyue it. The signifying lambe was offred at their Easter: and the Apostle Paule saith in the epistle of this present day, that Christ is our Easter, who was offred for vs, and on thys day rose from deathe.

The Israelites did eate the lambes fleshe, as God commaunded, wyth vnleuened bread, and wilde lettisse: *and we should receyue the holy housell of Christes bodye and bloud without the leauen of synne and iniquitie. As leauen turneth the creatures from theyr nature; so doth synne also chaunge the nature of man from innocencye to foule spottes of gyltinesse. The Apostle hath taught how wee should feast not in the leuen of iuelnesse, but in the swete dough of puritie and truthe.

* How we shoulde come to the holy communion.

The herbe whiche they shoulde eate wyth the vnleauened bread is called lettisse, and is bitter in taste. So we shoulde with bytternesse of vnfayned weepynge purifye our mynde, if we wil eat Christes body.

The Israelites were not wont to eate rawe fleshe; although God forbad them to eate it rawe, and sodden in water, but rosted wyth fyer. He will receyue the bodye of God rawe, that shal thynke wythout reason that Christ was onelye man lyke vnto vs, and was not God. And he that will after mans wisdome search of the misterie of Christes incarnation, doth lyke vnto hym that doth seeth lambes flesh in water: bycause that water in this place signifieth manes vnderstanding: but we should vnderstand that all the misteries of Christs humanity were ordered by the power of the Holy Ghost. And then eate we

In die Sancto Pascæ.

⁊ soþfæstnysse; Lactúca hatte seo
wyrt ðe hi etan sceoldon mid ðam
ðeorfum hlafum. heo is biter on ðigene;
⁊ þe sceolon mid biternysse soþre
behreopsunge ure mod geclænsian. gif
þe pillað Cristes lichaman ðicgan;

Næs þ Israhela folc gewunod. to
hreapum flæsce. ðeah ðe God him
bebude. þ hi hit hreap ne æton. ne on
pætere gesoden. ac gebræd to sire;
Se þile ðicgan Godes lichaman hreapne·
se þe buton gesceade penð þ he þære
anfeald man us gelic. ⁊ næse God;
And se ðe æfter mennircum pirdome
pyle smeagan ymbe ða geryno Cristes
flæschcnysse. he deþ spylce he seoþe
ðæs lambes flærc on pætere. forþan
þe pæter getacnaþ on ðissere stope
mennisc ingehid; Ac þe sceolon pitan
þ ealle ða geryno Cristes menniscnysse
pæron gefadode ðurh mihte ðæs halgan

In die Sancto Pascæ.

Gastes. ðonne dicge þe his lichaman gebræðne to fine. forðan ðe se halga Gast com on fyres hipe to ðam apostolum on mystlicum geseoriðum;

Issrahel sceolde etan þæs lambes heafod. ꝛ ða fet. ꝛ þ innepearde. ꝛ ðæs nan ðing belifan ne moste ofer niht; gif ðæs hpæt belife. forbærne man þ on fyre. ꝛ ne tobræcan ða baan; Æfter gastlicum andgite þe etaþ þæs lambes heafod. ðonne þe underfoþ Cristes godcundnysse on usum geleafan; Eft ðonne þe his mennyscnysse mid lufe underfoþ. þonne ete þe þæs lambes fet. forþan ðe Crist is angin and ende. God æs ealle þorulða. ꝛ man on ðissere þorulðe geendunge; Þpæt is ðæs lambes innepearde buton Cristes ðigelan beboðu. þa þe etaþ þonne þe lifes poð mid gnæðignysse underfoþ;

Nan þing ne moste þæs lambes beli

his body rosted with fyre: because the Holy Ghost came in fyrye likenes to the apostles in diuers tonges.

The Israelites should eate the lambs head, and the fete, and the purtenaunce, and nothing therof must be left ouer night. If any thing thereof were lefte, they should burne that in the fire: and they should not breake the bones. After ghostly vnderstanding we doe then eate the lambes head, when we take hold of Christs diuinitye in our beleife. Agayn when we take holde of his humanyte wyth loue, then eate we the lambes feete; bycause that Christ is the begynnyng and ende, God before all world, and man in the end of thys worlde. What be the lambes purtenaunce, but Christes secrete preceptes? and these we eat when we receiue with gredines the worde of lyfe.

There must nothing of the lambe be

left vnto the morning, bicause that al Godes sayings are to be searched with great carefulnesse: so that all his preceptes maye be knowen in vnderstanding and deede in the nyght of thys present lyfe, before that the last day of the vniuersall resurrection doe appeare. If we can not search out throughly all the mistery of Christes incarnation, then ought we to betake the rest vnto the might of the holy Ghost with true humilitie, and not searche to rashly of the depe secretnes aboue the measure of our vnderstanding.

They did eat the lambes flesh with their loynes gyrt. In the loines is the lust of the body; and he whyche wyll receyue the housell, shall restrayne concupiscence, and take with chastitie the holy receypt. They were also shod. What be shoes but of the hydes of dead beastes? We be truely shod, if we folow

In die Sancto Pascæ.

ꝼan oþ meꞃiȝen. ꝼoꞃþan þe Goðeꞃ cpýðaꞃ ꞃinð to aꞃmeaȝenne mið miceliꞃe caꝼꞃulnýꞃꞃe. ꞃpa ꝥ ealle hiꞃ beboða mið anðȝite anð peoꞃce beon aꞃmeaðe on mihte þiꞃeꞃ anðpeaꞃðan liꝼeꞃ. æꝼþan þe ꞃe enðenexta ðæȝ þæꞃ ȝemænelican æꝼiꞃteꞃ æteopiȝe; Giꝼ pe þonne ealle þa ȝeꞃýnu Cꞃiꞃteꞃ ꝼlæꞃchcnýꞃꞃe þuꞃhꞃmeaȝan ne maȝon. ðonne ꞃceole pe þa laꝼe betæcan þæꞃ halȝan ȝaꞃteꞃ mihte mið ꞃoþꞃe eaðmoðnýꞃꞃe. anð na to ðýꞃꞃtelice ýmbe ða ðeopan diȝelnýꞃꞃe oꝼeꞃ uꞃeꞃ anðȝýteꞃ mæþe ꞃmeaȝan;

Þi æton ꝥ lamb mið beȝýꞃðum lenðenum; On lenðenum iꞃ ꞃeo ȝalnýꞃ ðæꞃ lichoman. ꝥ ꞃe þe pýle ꝥ huꞃel ðicȝan he ꞃceal ȝeꝼꞃýþan þa ȝalnýꞃꞃe. ꝥ mið clænnýꞃꞃe ða halȝan þiȝene onꝼon; Þi pæꞃon eac ȝeꞃceoðe; Þpæt ꞃinð ȝeꞃcý buton ðeaðꞃa nýtena hýða; Þe beoþ ꞃoþlice ȝeꞃceoðe. ȝiꝼ pe eꝼenlæcaþ

In die Sancto Pascæ.

mid unum ꞅæpelde ⁊ peopce ꞅopþꞅa-
penꞅa manna lıꞅ. ðæꞅa ðe Gode ge-
þugon þuꞅh gehealdꞅumnẏꞅꞅe hıꞅ beboda;

Þı hæꞅdon hım ꞅtæꞅ on handa æt
þæꞅe þıgene; Se ꞅtæꞅ getacnaþ gẏmene
⁊ hẏꞅdnẏꞅꞅe; Þa þe bet cunnon ⁊
magon. ꞅceolon gẏman oþꞅa manna. ⁊
mıd heoꞅa ꞅultume undeꞅꞅꞅeþıan; Þam
gemettum pæꞅ beboden þ hı ꞅceoldon
cáꞅlıce etan. ꞅopþam ðe God onꞅcunað
ða ꞅleacnẏꞅꞅe on hıꞅ ðegnum. ⁊ þa he
luꞅaþ ðe mıd modeꞅ caꞅneꞅꞅe ðæꞅ ecan
lıꞅeꞅ mıꞅhþe ꞅecaþ; Þıt ıꞅ apꞅıten.
Ne elca ðu to gecẏꞅꞅanne to Gode.
ðẏlæꞅ þe ꞅe tıma loꞅıe þuꞅh þa ꞅleacan
elcunge;

Þa gemettan ne moꞅton ðæꞅ lambeꞅ
bán ꞅcænan. ne ða cempan ðe Cꞅıꞅt
ahengon ne moꞅton tobꞅæcan hıꞅ halgan ꞅceancan. ꞅpa ꞅpa hı dẏdon þæꞅa

in our steppes and dedes, the lyfe of those pilgrimes, which pleased God with keping of his commaundements.

They had staues in their handes when they ate. The stafe signifieth a carefulnes and a diligent ouerseing; and al they that best know and can, should take care of other men, and staye them vppe wyth their helpe. It was inioyned to the eaters that they should eate the lambe in haste. For God abhorreth slothfulnes in his seruauntes; and those he loueth that seeke the ioye of euerlasting life with quicknes of minde. It is written: Prolong not to turne vnto God, lest the time passe awaye through thy slowe tarrying.

The eaters might not breake the lambes bones. No more mought the souldyers that did hang Christ breake his holy legges, as they did of the two theefes that hanged on either syde of him. And the Lord rose from death sound without al corruption: and at the last iudgement they shall see him, whom they did most cruelly wounde on the crosse.

This time is called in the Ebrue tonge Pasca, and in Latine Transitus, and in English a Passouer; bicause that on this daye the people of Israell passed from the land of Ægipt ouer the read sea: from bondage to the land of promyse.

So also dyd our Lord at thys tyme departe, as sayeth Iohn the Euangelyste, from thys world to his heauenly Father. Euen so we ought to folowe our head, and to go from the deuill to Christ, from this vnstable world to his stable kingdome. Howbeit we should first in this present life depart from vices to holy vertues, from euil manners to good manners, if we will after this corruptible

In die Sancto Pascæ. 53

tpezna sceaþena. ðe him on tpa healfa hanzoðon. ac Dpihten apas of deaþe zesund buton ælcepe sopnotoðnýsse; And hi sceolon zeseon æt ðam micclan dome. hpæne hi zepundoðon pælhpeoplice on poðe;

Þeos tið is zehaten on ebpeiscum zepeopðe Pasca. þ is on leden Tpansitus. J on Enzlisc Fæpelð. sopþan þe on þisum dæze sepðe Goðes folc fpam Ezipta lanðe open þa peaðan sæ. fpam þeopte to þam behatenan eapðe;

Upe Dpihten sepðe eac on þispe timan. spa spa se Goðspellepe Iohannes cpæþ. fpam þisum ...ioðan-eapðe to his heofonlican fæðep, Þe sceolon fýlian upum heapðe. J sapan fpam deople to Cpiste. fpam þissepe unstæþþizan populðe. to his staþelsæstan pice. ac pe sceolon æpest. on upum anðpeapðan lise. sapan fpam leahtpum to halzum mæznum. fpam unþeapum to zóðum

þeapum. ᵹiꝼ pe pillað. æꝼteꞃ ðiꞃum
lænan liꝼe. ꝼaꞃan to þam ecan. ⁊ æꝼteꞃ
uꞃum æꞃiꞃte. to hælenðe Cꞃiꞃte; Þe
uꞃ ᵹelæðe to hiꞃ liꝼiᵹenðan Fæðeꞃ. ðe
hine ꞃealðe ꝼoꞃ uꞃum ꞃynnum to ðeaþe;
Si him pulðoꞃ ⁊ loꝼ ðæꞃe pelðæðe. on
ealꞃa pobulða pobulð; AMEN :·

life go to the eternal life; and, after our resurrection, to Jesus Christ. He bring vs to his euerliuing Father, who gaue him to death for our sinnes. To him be honour, and praise of the wel doing, world wythout ende. Amen.

This Sermon is found in diuerse
bookes of Sermons written in the olde
Englishe or Saxon Tounge: whereof two bookes bee now in the
handes of the most reue-
rend Father the Arch-
bishop of Caunter-
burye.

Here followeth the wordes
of Elfrike Abbot of S. Albons, and
also of Malmesberye, taken out of
his Epistle written to Wvlfsine Byshop
of Scyrburne. It is founde in a
booke of the olde Saxon tounge,
wherein be xliij. chapters of Canons
and ecclesiasticall constitutions, and
also Liber pœnitentialis, that is,
a pœnitentiall booke, or shryfte
booke, deuided into iiij. other
bokes: the Epistle is set for
the 30. chapter of the
fourth boke, intituled be pneoꞅt‑
ꞅinoþe, that is, concerning a Synode
of priestes: and this epistle
is also in a Canon boke
of the churche
of Exeter.

Epistola ad Wulfsinum.

Sume preostas healdað ðæt husel ðe bið on Eastep-dæg gehalgod ofer geap to seocum mannum. ac hi mispoþ swyþe deope. þ ðæt halige husel sceole fynegian. ꞅ nellaþ undepstandan hu mycele dædbote seo pœnitentialis tæcþ be þam. gif ðæt husel biþ fynig. oþþe hæþen. oþþe gif hit foplopen bið. oþþe gif mys oþþe nytenu ðuph gymelease hit etaþ; Man sceal healdan ðæt halige husel mid micelre gymene ꞅ ne fophealdan hit. ac halgian oðep ednipe to seocum mannum. á embe seofon niht. oððe embe feopertyne niht. þ hit hunu fynig ne sy. fop ðon þe eal swa halig bið þ husel þe nu to-dæg pær gehalgod. swa þ þe on eastep-dæg pær gehalgod;

Ðæt husel is Cristes lichama na lichamlice ac gastlice; Na se lichama ðe he on ðropode. ac se lichama ðe he

Epistle to Wulfsine.

SOME pristes keepe the housell that is hallowed on Easter-day all the yere for syke men. But they do greatelye amysse, bycause it waxeth horye and rotten. And these wyll not vnderstand how greuous penaunce the pœnitentiall booke teacheth by thys, if the housell become horye or rotten, or yf it bee lost, or be eaten of myse or beastes by neglygence. Men shal reserue more carefullye the holy housell, and not reserue it to longe, but hallowe other of newe for sycke men alwayes wythin a weke or a fortnight, that it be not so much as horye. For so holy is the housell which to-day is hallowed, as that whyche on Easter daye was hallowed.

The housell is Christes bodye, not bodylye, but ghostlye. Not the body which he suffred in, but the bodye of

which he spake, when he blessed bread
and wyne to housell a night before his
suffring, and sayd by the blessed breade,
thys is my bodye; and agayne by the
hallowed wyne, this is my bloude,
whiche is shedd for manye in forgeuenes of sinnes.

Vnderstand nowe that the Lord, who
could turne the bread before his suffring to his body, and the wyne to his
bloude ghostlye; that the selfe same
Lorde blesseth dayly throughe the
priestes handes bread and wine to his
ghostly body, and to his ghostly bloud.

Here thou seest (good Reader) how Elfrike vpon
fynding fault wyth an abuse of his tyme, which was,
that priestes on Easter day filled their housell boxe,
and so kept the bread a whole yere for sick men,
toke an occasion to speake agaynst the bodely pre-

embe ſpɲæc. ða ða he bletſobe hlaf
anb pın to huſ'le anɲe nıhte æɲ hıſ'
ðɲopunʒe. ꝸ cpæþ be ðam ʒebletſoban
hlafe. ðıſ' ıſ' mın lıchama. ꝸ eft be ðam
ʒehalʒoban pıne. ðıſ' ıſ' mın blob. þe
bıþ foɲ maneʒum aʒoten on ſ'ẏnna foɲ-
ʒẏfenneſſe;

Unbeɲſtanbaþ nu ꝥ ſe Dɲıhten. ðe
mıhte apenban ðone hlaf æɲ hıſ' ðɲopunʒe to hıſ' lıchaman. anb ꝥ pın to
hıſ' blobe ʒaſtlıce. ðæt ſe ẏlca bæʒ-
hpamlıce bletſaþ. ðuɲh ſaceɲıba hanba.
hlaf ꝸ pın. to hıſ' ʒaſtlıcan lıchaman. ꝸ
to hıſ' ʒaſtlıcan blobe;

sence of Christ in the Sacrament. So also in another
epistle sent to Wulfstane, Archbyshop of Yorke, hee
reprehending agayn thys ouerlong reseruing of the
housell, addeth also wordes more at large against the
same bodely presence. His words be these:

Sume preostas gefyllaþ heora husel-
box on eastron. ⁊ healdað oþer tƿelf
monaþ to untrumum mannum. sƿylce
ðæt husel sy haligre þonne oþer; Ac
hi doð unrihtlice. forþam þe hit þannaþ.
oþþe mid ealle forrotaþ on swa langum
fyrste. ⁊ he bið ðonne scyldig. swa swa
us segþ seo boc; Se ðe husel forhylt.
oþþe hit forlyst. oþþe mys eton. oþþe
oþre nytenu. sceapa þa pœnitentialem.
hƿæt he sægþ be þisum; Eall swa halig
is ðæt husel ðe bið gehalgod to-dæg.
swa ðæt ðe biþ gehalgod on þam halgan
eastor-dæge; Healdað forþig. ic bidde.
ðone halgan Cristes lichaman mid
maran wisdome to seocum mannum
fram sunnan dæge to sunnan dæge on
swiðe clænum boxe. oððe be ðam
mæstan feoƿertyne niht. and dicgað
hit ðonne. and lecgaþ ðær oþer;

Ƿe habbaþ bysene be þam on Moyses

SOME priests fil their boxe for housel on Easter day, and so reserue it a whole yere for sicke men, as though that housel were more holy then any other. But they doe vnaduisedlye, bicause it waxeth hory, or al together rotten by keping it so long space. And thus is he become giltie, as the boke wytnesseth to vs. Yf anye do keepe the housell to long, or lose it, or myse, or other beasts do eate it, see what the pœnitential boke sayeth by this. So holy is altogether that housell, which is hallowed to-daye, as that which is hallowed on Easter day. Wherefore I besech you to kepe the holy bodye of Christ with more aduisement for sick men, from sonday to sonday, in a very cleane boxe: or at the most, not to kepe it aboue a fortnight, and then eate it, laying other in the place.

Wee haue an example hereof in

Moyses bookes, as God him selfe hath commaunded in Moyses lawe: How the priestes should set on euery saturnday twelfe loues al newe baked in the tabernacle; the whyche were called panes propositionis: and those should stand there in Gods tabernacle, till the next saturnday, and then did the pristes them selues eate them, and set other in the place.

Some priestes wil not eate the housell, which they do hallow. But we will now declare vnto you how the boke speaketh by them. Presbyter missam celebrans, et non audens sumere sacrificium, accusante conscientia sua, anathema est: The priste that doth say masse, and dare not eate the housell, hys conscience accusynge hym, is accursed. It is lesse daunger to receyue the housell, then to hallowe it. He that doth twise hallow one host to housell, is lyke vnto the

bocum. swa swa God sylf bebead on
Moyses æ. ðæt se sacerd sceolde. on
ælcum sæternes dæge. settan twelf
hlafas on ðam tabernaculo. ealle niwe
bacene. ða wæron gehatene panes propositionis. and his sceoldon ðær stand-
an on ðam Godes getælde oþ oðerne
sæternes dæg. and etan hi ðonne ða
sacerdas sylfe. and settan ðær oþre;

Sume preostas nellað ðicgan ðæt
husel ðe hi halgiaþ; Nu wille we eow
secgan. hu seo boc segþ be þam;
Presbyter missam celebrans. et non
audens sumere acrificium. accusante
conscientia sua. anathema est; Se
mæsse preost ðe mæssaþ. and ne dear
ðæt husel ðicgan. pat hine scyldigne.
se is amansumod; Læsse pleoh is to
þicgenne ðæt husel. þonne to halgienne;
Se þe tuwa halgaþ ane ofletan to husle.

ſe biþ þam ᵹeðpolan ᵹelice. þe an cilð
fullaþ cupa;

Cpiſt ſẏlf ᵹehalᵹoðe huſel æp hiſ
þpopunᵹe. he bletſoðe þone hlaf. anð
tobpæc. þuſ cpeþenðe to hiſ halᵹum
apoſtolum; Etaþ þiſne hlaf. hit iſ
min lichama. anð he eft bletſoðe ænne
calic mið pine. anð cpæþ heom þuſ to;
Dpincaþ ealle of þiſum. hit iſ min aᵹen
bloð þæpe nipan ᵹecẏþnẏſſe. þe biþ for
manᵹum aᵹoten on ſẏnna forᵹẏfe-
nẏſſe; Se Dpihten þe halᵹoðe huſel
æp hiſ þpopunᵹe. anð cpæþ ꝥ ſe hlaf
pæpe hiſ aᵹen lichama. anð þæt pin
pæpe pitoðlice hiſ bloð. ſe halᵹaþ dæᵹ-
hpamlice þuph hiſ ſacepða hanða hlaf
to hiſ lichaman. anð pin to hiſ bloð
on ᵹaſtlicepe ᵹepẏne. ſpa ſpa pe ræðaþ
on bocum;

Ne bið ſe liflica hlaf lichamlice ſpaþeah ſe ẏlca lichama. ðe Cpiſt on

heretike, who doth christen twyse one childe. [Baptizes a child twice.]

Christ him selfe blessed housel before his suffring : he blessed the bread, and brake, thus speaking to his apostels: Eate this bread, it is my body. And agayne he blessed one chalice with wyne, and thus also speaketh vnto them: Drinke ye all of this: it is myne owne bloud of the newe testament, which is shed for many in forgeuenes of synnes. The Lord which halowed housell before his suffering, and sayeth, that the bread was his owne body, and that the wyne was truly his bloud, he haloweth dayly, by the handes of the prist, bread to his body, and wyne to his bloud, in ghostly mystery; as we read in bokes.

And yet that liuely bread is not bodely so notwithstanding: not the self same body that Christ suffered in. Nor is that holy wine the Sauiours bloud which was shed for vs, in bodely thing, but in ghostly vnderstanding. Both be truly the bread hys body, and the wyne also hys bloud, as was the heauenly bread, which we call Manna, that fed forty yeres Gods people. And the cleare water which did then runne from the stone in the wildernes, was truly his bloud; as Paul wrote in summe of his epistles: Omnes patres nostri eandem escam spiritualem manducauerunt, et omnes eundem potum spiritualem biberunt, &c. All our fathers ate in the wildernes the same ghostlye meate, and dranke the same ghostly drinke. They dranke of that gostly stone, and that stone was Christ. The apostle hath said as you now haue heard, that they all did eate the same ghostly meate, and they all did drinke the same ghostly

þropode; Ne þæt haliȝe pin nir þær hælendes blod þe for us aȝoten pær on lichamlican þinȝe. ac on ȝastlicum and-ȝyte; Æȝþer biþ soþlice se hlaf his lichama. and þ pin eac his blod. swa swa se heofonlica hlaf pær. þe þe hataþ manna. ðe feopertiȝ ȝeara afedde Godes folc. and ðæt hlutre pæter pær pitodlice his blod. þe arn of ðam stane on ðam pestene ða; Swa swa Paulus apnat on sumon his pistole; Omnes patres nostri eandem escam spiritualem manducauerunt. et omnes eundem potum spiritualem biberunt. &c.; Ealle ure fæderas æton on þam pestene þone ylcan ȝastlican mete. and þone ȝastlican drenc druncon; Þi druncon of þam ȝastlican stane. and se stan pær Crist; Se apostol sæde swa swa ȝe nu ȝehyrdon. ðæt hi ealle æton ðone ylcan ȝastlican mete. ꝥ hi

ealle ðruncon ðone gaſtlican drenc;
Ne cpæþ he na lichamlice. ac gaſtlice;
Næſ Cpiſt ða gyt geboren. ne hiſ blod
næſ agoten. þa þæt Iſrahela folc gæt
ðone mete. and oſ þam ſtane dranc.
and ſe ſtan næſ lichamlice Cpiſt. þeah
he ſpa cpæde; Hit pæron þa ylcan
gerynu on þære ealdan æ. ꞇ hi gaſtlice
getacnodon þæt gaſtlice huſel uref
hælendeſ lichaman. þe þe halgiaþ nu :.

drinke. And hee sayth not bodely, but ghostly. And Christ was not yet borne, nor hys bloud shedde, when that the people of Israell ate that meat, and dranke of that stone. And the stone was not bodelye Christ, though he so sayd. It was the same misteries in the olde law, and they did ghostlye signifie that ghostly housell of our Sauiours body, which we consecrate now.

THIS Epistle to Wulfstane Elfrike wrote first in the Latyne tounge, as in a short Latyne Epistle set before this, and one other of hys Saxon Epistles, he confesseth thus: Ælfricus Abbas Wulfstano venerabili Archiepiscopo salutem in Christo. Ecce paruimus vestræ almitatis iussionibus transferentes Anglice duas Epistolas quas Latino eloquio descriptas ante annum vobis destinauimus; non tamen semper ordinem sequentes, nec verbum ex verbo, sed sensum ex sensu proferentes. Behold we haue obeyed the commaundement of thy excellencie in translating into Englishe the two Epistles which we sent vnto thee, written in Latine more than a yeare agoe. Howbeit we keepe not here alwayes the same order; nor yet translate worde for worde, but sense for sense. Nowe because verye fewe there be that doe vnderstande the old Englishe or Saxon (so much is our speech chaunged from the vse of that time, wherein Elfrike liued) and for that also it maye be that some will doubt how skilfullye and also faythfullye these wordes of Elfrike be translated from the Saxon tounge: wee haue thought good to set downe here last of all the very wordes also of his Latyne epistle, which is recorded in bokes fayre wrytten of olde in the Cathedrall Churches of Worcester and Excester.

QVIDAM vero Presbyteri implent alabastrum suum de sacrificio, quod in Pasca Domini sanctificant : et conseruant per totum annum ad infirmos, quasi sanctior sit cæteris sacrificijs. Sed nimium insipienter faciunt. Quia nigrescit, et putrescit tamdiu conseruatum. Et liber pœnitentialis pro tali negligentia pœnitentiam magnam docet: aut si a muribus commestum sit : aut ab auibus raptum. Tam sanctum est sacrificium, quod hodie sanctificatur, quam illud quod in die Pascæ consecratum est. Et ideo debetis à dominica in dominicam, aut per duos, vel maximè tres hebdomadas tenere sacrificium in alabastro mundo ad infirmos : ne nigrescat, aut putrescat, si diutiùs seruetur. Nam in lege Moisi ponebant sacerdotes semper omni sabbato panes propositionis calidos in tabernaculo coram Domino : et in sequenti sabbato sumebant illos soli sacerdotes, et edebant: et alios nouos pro eis ponebant. Facite et vos sacerdotes similiter.

Custodite cautè sacrificium Christi ad infirmos, et edite illud, ne diutius teneatur, quam oportet. Et reponite aliud nouiter sanctificatum propter necessitatem infirmorum, ne sine viatico exeant de hoc seculo. Christus Iesus in die suæ sanctæ cœnæ accepit panem: benedixit, ac fregit: dedit discipulis suis dicens, Accipite, et comedite. Hoc est enim corpus meum. Similiter et calicem accipiens gratias egit, et dedit illis dicens, Bibite ex hoc omnes. Hic est sanguis meus noui Testamenti, qui pro multis effundetur in remissionem peccatorum. Intelligite modo sacerdotes, quod ille Dominus qui ante passionem suam potuit conuertere illum panem, et illud vinum ad suum corpus et sanguinem: quod ipse quotidie sanctificat per manus sacerdotum suorum panem ad suum corpus spiritualiter, et vinum ad suum sanguinem.

(Non fit tamen hoc sacrificium corpus eius in quo passus est pro nobis: neque sanguis eius, quem pro nobis effudit: sed spiritualiter corpus eius efficitur et sanguis: sicut manna quod de cœlo pluit, et aqua quæ de petra fluxit. Sicut Paulus Apostolus ait), Nolo enim vos ignorare fratres, quoniam patres nostri omnes sub nube fuerunt: et omnes mare transierunt: et omnes in Moysi baptizati sunt in nube et in mari. Et omnes eandem escam spiritualem manducauerunt: et omnes eundem potum spiritualem biberunt. Bibebant autem de spirituali consequenti eos petra. Petra autem erat Christus. Vnde dicit Psalmista, Panem cœli dedit eis. Panem angelorum manducauit

---

( ) The words inclosed betwene the ij. halfe circles, some had rased out of Worceter booke, but they are restored agayne out of a booke of Exeter Church.

homo. Nos quoque proculdubio manducamus panem angelorum: et bibimus de illa petra, quæ Christum significabat: quotiens fideliter accedimus ad sacrificium corporis et sanguinis Christi.

THE LORDS PRAYER, THE CREEDE,

AND

THE TEN COMMAUNDEMENTS

IN THE

SAXON AND ENGLISHE TOUNGE.

THAT it is no new thyng to teache the people of God the Lordes prayer, and the articles of their beliefe in the Englishe tounge, wherby they mought the better serue their God, and holde faste their profession of Christianitie: may well bee proued by many godly decrees of byshops, and lawes of kinges, made from tyme to tyme in the reigne of the Saxons, before the Conquest. In a councell holden by Cuthbert Archbyshop of Canterburye, in the yeare of our Lorde 747. and in the 33. yeare of Æthelbalde king of Mercia (who was present at this same Councell with his princes and dukes) it was decreed*, Vt ipsi presbyteri dominicam orationem et simbolum anglice discant et doceant: That the priestes doe both learne them selues, and also teach to others, the Lordes prayer and the Creede in Englishe.

In old Canon bokes of Churches, & in the epistles of Ælfricke, we read it thus inioyned to priestes: Se mæſſe-pṛeoſt ſceal ſecᵹan on ſunnandaᵹum and mæſſe-daᵹum ðæſ ᵹodſpelleſ and-ᵹẏt on enᵹliſc ðam ſolce· and be ðam Paten noſten ⁊ be ðam Cṛedan eac· ſpa he oſtoſt mæᵹe· þam mannum to onbṛẏṛdnẏſſe· ꝥ hı cunnon ᵹeleaſan ⁊ heoṛa cṛıſtendom ᵹehaldan; The priest shall say vnto the people on sondayes and holydayes, the sense of the

---

* William of Malms. 1. lib. de Pontificibus.

Gospell in Englishe: and so also touching the Lordes prayer, and the Creede, so oft as he may, to mens contrition, that they may know their beleefe, and keepe sure their Christianitie.

Cnut a King of England worthie of memorie, amongest many other good lawes he made in the time of his princely gouernment, hath also thys law: And ealle cɼıꞅtene men þe lænaþ ꞅpıþe ᵹeoɼne. þæt hıᵹ ınpeaɼðɼe heoɼtan æꝼɼe God luꝼıan. and ɼıhtne cɼıꞅtendom ᵹeoɼnlıc healdan. and ᵹodcundan laɼeoþan ᵹeoɼnlıce hyɼan. ⁊ Godeꞅ laɼa ⁊ laᵹa ꞅmeaᵹan oꝼt ⁊ ᵹelome hım ꞅylꝼum to þeaɼꝼe; And þe lænaþ þ ælc cɼıꞅten man ᵹeleoɼnıᵹe þ he huɼu cunne ɼıhtne ᵹeleaꝼan aɼıht undeɼꞅtandan. and Pateɼ noꞅteɼ ⁊ Cɼedan ᵹeleoɼnıan. ꝼoɼ ðam mıd þam oþɼum ꞅceal ælc cɼıꞅten mann hıne to Gode ᵹebıddan. ⁊ mıd þam oþɼum ᵹeꞅputelıan ɼıhtne ᵹeleaꝼan; We admonish diligently all Christian men, that they doe alwayes loue God with an inwarde harte, and hold earnestly right Christendome, and be diligently obedient to deuine teachers, and doe subtilly search Gods learning and lawes often and daily to the profit of themselues: And we warne that all Christian men doe learne to know at the least wyse the right beliefe, and aright to vnderstand; and learne the Pater noster, and the Creede. For that with the one euery Christian man shall pray vnto God, and with the other shewe forth right beliefe.

Thus is it reserued in memorie, & put in writing, as touching the diligent care that the former age of the Church of God had to haue the people of God well instructed in that prayer, whereof Christ him self is the author, and in the articles of their beliefe. Which prayer of the Lord, and Creede, with the tenne lawlike wordes, that God him self taught

Moyses, and wrote with his finger in
two tables of stone on the mount Sinai
for all mens chastisement, as well for
that olde people that was in tymes
paste, as also for vs that bee now: be
here set out as they are yet sene in
old bokes of the Saxon tonge.
But for the better vnderstanding
of any worde that may seeme
harde vnto the reader, we
haue thought good to
place ouer the Sax-
on the familiar
wordes of our
own speech.

Matth. 6.

Verely when ye pray nyll ye
Soþlice ðonne ge gebiddon. nellon ge

speake much as the hethen. They
sppæcan fela swa swa hæþene; Þis

thinke that they be harde in their
penaþ ðæt hig syn gehýrede on heora

manyfolde speaking. Nill ye
manigfealdan sppæce; Nellon ge

therefore them do like vnto. Verely
eornostlice him geefenlæcan; Soþlice

your father wote what your nede is,
eoper fæder pat hpæt eop ðearf is.

before that ye hym pray. Wher-
ærþam ðe ge hine biddaþ; Eornost-

fore praye ye thus:
lice gebiddaþ eop ðus;

The Lordes praier
Pater noster
in Englishe:
on Engliſc.

THOU our father which art in heauen, be thy name hallowed. Come thy kingdome. Be thy will in earth, as in heauen. Geue vs to-day our daylye bread. And forgeue vs our trespasses, as we forgeue them that against vs trespasse. And ne lead thou not vs into temptation. But deliuer vs from euill. Be it so.

ÐU ure fæder ðe eart on heouenum· ſi þin nama gehalgod. Cume þin rice; Si ðin pilla on eorþan· ſpa ſpa on heoronum; Syle uſ to-dæg urne dæghpamlican hlaf; And forgif uſ ure gyltaſ· ſpa ſpa pe forgifaþ ðam ðe piþ uſ agyltaþ; And ne læd ðu na uſ on coſtnunge; Ac alyſ uſ fram yfele; Si hit ſpa :·

The Beliefe in English:
Creðo in Deum on Englisc.

I beleue in God the Father Almigh-
Ic gelýfe on God fæder ælmih-

tye, maker of heauen and earth.
tigne. scyppend heofenan ꝧ eorþan;

And I beleue in the Sauiour Christ his
ꝧ ic gelýfe on Hælend Crist his

onely begotten Sonne our Lorde, who
ancennedan sunu urne Drihten. se

was conceaued of the Holy Ghost,
þæs geeacnod of ðam halgan gaste.

and borne of Marye the virgyne,
ꝧ acenned of Marian ðam mædene.

suffred vnder the Pontish Pilate,
geþrowod under þam Pontiscan Pilate.

on the crosse hanged, he was dead, and
on rode ahangen. he þæs dead. ꝧ

buryed, and he down descended to hel.
bebyrged. ꝧ he nyðer astah to helle;

And he arose from death on the thyrd
⁊ he aras of deaþe on þā þriddan

daye. And he went vp to heauen,
dæge ; And he astah up to heofonum.

and sitteth now at the right hand of God
and sitt nu æt swiðran Godes

Almightie the Father. From thence he will
ælmihtiges fæder ; Ðanon he wile

come to iudge both the quicke
cuman to demenne ægþer ge ða cucum.

and the deade. And I beleue on
ge þam deadum ; And ic gelyfe on

the Holy Ghost. And the holy Con-
þone halgan gast ; And ða halgan ge-

gregation. And of the saintes the societie.
laþunge ;   ⁊ halgena gemænnysse ;

And sins forgeuenesse. And of the flesh
⁊ synna forgifenysse ; ⁊ flæsces

the again-rising. And the euerlasting life.
ærist ;   ⁊ þ   ece life :·

The ten commaundements which also God
Ða tẏn beboda ðe eac God

himselfe proclaimed from the mounte with
sylf geclẏpode of þam munte mid

loude voyce to all the men
micelre stemne to eallum ðam mannum

which with Moyses were in the wilder-
ðe mid Moyse pæron on ðam pæst-

nesse then.
ene ða;

The Lorde was speaking these wordes to
Dryhten pær sprecende ðas word to

Moyses, and thus sayde: I am the Lord
Moyse. and ðus cpæþ. Ic eom Dryhten

thy God, I thee out ledde of Ægypt
ðin God. Ic ðe ut gelædde of Egipta

lande, and of their bondage. Ne
londe. and of hiora ðeopdome; Ne

loue thou other straunge Gods besides me.
lufa ðu oþre fremde Godas ofer me;

Ne my name call thou in vayne:
Ne minne noman ne ciȝ ðu on ıdelneſſe.

for that thou ne arte guiltlesse with
forþon ðe ðu ne bıſt unſcýldıȝ pıþ

me, if thou in vayne callest my
me. ȝıf ðu on ıdelneſſe cıȝſt minne

name. Remember that thou hallowe
noman; Gemýne þ ðu ȝehalȝıȝe

the rest-day. Worke you six
ðone ræſte-dæȝ; Pýnceaþ eop ſýx

dayes, and on the seuenth rest you:
daȝaſ. ꝸ on þam ſıofoþan reſtaþ eop.

bycause in six dayes Christ made
forðam on ſýx daȝum Cpıſt ȝeporhte

heauen and earth, the sea, and all
heofonaſ. ꝸ eorþan. ſæſ. and ealle

creatures that in them be. And him
ȝeſceafta ðe on hım ſınt; ꝸ hıne

rested on the seuenth day: and ther-
ȝereſte on þone ſıofoþan dæȝ. ꝸ for-

fore the Lord it hallowed. Honour
þon Dryhten hine gehalgod; Ara
thy father and thy mother, that
ðynum fæder. J þinre meddeɹ. ða ðe
the Lorde gaue thee, that thou be
Dryhten sealde ðe. Þ ðu sie
the longer lyuing in the earth. Ne
ðy lenge libbende on eorþan; Ne
kill thou. Ne* lighe thou priuely.
sleah ðu; Ne* lige þu dearnenga;
Ne steale thou. Ne say thou false
Ne stala ðu; Ne sæge ðu lease
witnesse. Ne desire thou thy
gepitnesse; Ne pilna ðu ðynes
neighbours heritage with vnright.
nehstan ierfes mid unrihte :·

These Commaundements we haue
taken from the Lawes of Alfrede the
King, before which they are alwaies

* That is, commit no adultery.

placed: but here the manner of speaking in the Scripture is somewhat chaunged, and that more is, here is left out these words. (Non facies sculptile, neque omnem similitudinem quæ est in cœlo desuper, et quæ est in terra deorsum, nec eorum quæ sunt in aquis sub terra: non adorabis neque coles, &c. 2. Thou shalt not make to thy selfe any grauen Image, nor the likenesse of any thing that is in heauen aboue, or in the earth beneath, or in the water vnder the earth. Thou shalt not bowe downe to them, nor worship them. For I thy Lord &c.) Which thyng is done in all copyes of Alfredes lawes written in the Saxon tounge: and not onely in them, but in many other bookes, as hath beene seene, eyther Saxon or Lattyne, intreatyng of the commandementes, which were written before the Conquest, and since the second Nicene councell, wherein was decreed the worshipping of images. See what followed of taking away from the worde of God contrarye to the expresse commaundement of the same, vpon the vngodly decree of that councell.

When this thing was espied by them that translated these lawes into the Lattyne tounge sone after the Conquest, these words were restored agayne by the translatours to their due place, as by the Lattyne bookes of the lawes it is to be seene.

But bicause we haue made mention of that second Nicene councell whiche decreed both of the hauing and worshipping of Images, we shall here brieflye shewe what our stories report, was thought of the same councell by the learned of England, and chieflye by that great learned Englyshe man, and of most fame in that age, Alcuine, schoolemaister to Charles the great. Anno ab incarnatione Domini 792. Carolus rex Francorum misit Synodalem librum ad Britanniam sibi à Constantinopoli directum: in quo libro heu proh dolor! multa inconuenientia et veræ fidei contraria reperta sunt: maxime quod pene omnium orientalium doctorum, non minus quam trecentorum, vel eo amplius episcoporum vnanima assertione confirmatum imagines adorari debere: quod omnino ecclesia Dei execratur. Contra quod scripsit Alcuinus epistolā ex autoritate diuinarum scripturarum mirabiliter affirmatam, illamque cum eodem libro et persona episcoporum et principum nostrorum regi Francorum attulit. That is: In the yere from the incarnation of our Lord 792. Charles king of Fraunce sent to Brytaine a Synodebooke, which was directed vnto hym from Constantinople: in the which booke alas! many thinges vnconuenient and contrarye to the true fayth were found: in especiall, that it was establyshed with a whole consent almost of all the learned of the East, no lesse than of three hundred byshoppes or more, that men ought to worship Images, the whiche the Churche of God doth vtterlye abhorre. Agaynst the whiche Alcuine wrote an epistle wondrouslye proued by the authoritie of holy Scripture, and brought that epistle with the same booke, and names of our byshoppes and princes to the king of Fraunce.

  This storye hath Simeon
of Durham, Roger
Houeden, Flores
Historiarum, and
the Historie of
Rochester.

DE PETRO APOSTOLO.

Se Hælend þa cwæð. Hwæt secge ge þæt ic sy; Petrus him andwyrde. Þu eart Crist þæs lyfiendan Godes sunu; Drihten him cwæð to andsware. Eadig eart þu Simon culfran bearn ɼc...

Beda se trahtnere us onwrihð þa deopnysse þyssre rædinge; * * * *

Drihten cwæð to Petre. Þu eart stænen; For þære strencþe his geleafan. and for anrædnysse his andetnysse. he underfeng þone naman. forþan ðe he geþeodde hine sylfne mid fæstum mode to Criste. se þe is Stan gecweden fram þam apostole Paule;

And ic timbrie mine cyrcan uppon þysum stane. þæt is. ofer þam gelearan þe ðu andetst; Eall Godes gela-

OF THE APOSTLE PETER.

JESUS then said, "What say ye that I am?" Peter answered him, "Thou art Christ, the living God's Son." The Lord to him said for answer, "Blessed art thou, Simon, dove's child," &c. * * * * *

Bede the expounder unveils to us the deepness of this lesson. * * *

The Lord said to Peter, "Thou art rocken *."—For the strength of his faith, and for the firmness of his confession, he received that name; because he joined himself with steadfast mind to Christ, who is called a Rock by the apostle Paul.

"And I will build my church upon this rock;" that is, upon the faith

* Literally stonen, having the same relation to stone as rocken to rock, golden to gold, earthen to earth, &c.

which thou confessest. All God's convocation* is built upon the rock; that is, upon Christ; because he is the ground-wall† of all the structures of his own church.

All God's churches are accounted as one convocation; and this is built with chosen men, not with dead stones; and all the building of those lively stones is laid upon Christ; because we are, through faith, accounted his members, and he our 'aller'‡ head. Who[soever] builds off the ground-wall, his work shall fall, to [his] great loss.

Jesus said, "The gates of hell shall not have power against my church." Sins and erroneous doctrine are hell's gates, because they lead the sinful [man]

---

* Such is the nearest English for 'gelaðung,' from laðigan, to call, to invite.

† In modern orthography, the Saxon for 'foundation.'

‡ In the speech of Wiclif, Chaucer, and James the First of Scotland, "oure aller, oure alder, oure alleris," of us all.

ðunᵹ iſ oꝼeſi þam ſtane ᵹebẏtloð. þæt
iſ. oꝼeſi Cꞃiſte. ꝼoꞃþan ðe he iſ ſe
ᵹꞃunðpeal ealꞃa þæꞃa ᵹetimbꞃunᵹa hiſ
aᵹenꞃe cẏꞃcan;

Ealle Goðeſ cẏꞃcan ſinð ᵹetealðe to
anꞃe ᵹelaðunᵹe. anð ſeo iſ ᵹetimbꞃoð
mið ᵹecoꞃenum mannum. na mið beað-
um ſtanum. anð eall ſeo bẏtlunᵹ þæꞃa
liꝼliꞃa ſtana iſ oꝼeꞃ Cꞃiſte ᵹeloᵹoð.
ꝼoꞃþan ðe ꝼe beoð þuꞃh ðone ᵹeleaꝼan
hiſ lima ᵹetealðe. anð he uꞃe ealꞃa heaꝼoð; Se þe bẏtlað* oꝼ þam ᵹꞃunð-
pealle. hiſ peoꞃc hꞃẏſt to micclum lẏꞃe;

Se Pælenð cpæð. Ne maᵹon helle
ᵹatu naht toᵹeaneſ minꞃe cẏꞃcan;
Leahtꞃaſ anð ðpollice† laſ ſinð helle
ᵹatu. ꝼoꞃþan þe hi læðað þone ſẏnꝼullan

---

* Ne bytlað of, Ælfr. Soc. Hom.,—an incomplete negative, where a negative with "of" is a complete contradiction of the sense. "Of," off, or away from, is opposed to "ofer" and "uppon," and elegantly avoids a repetition of either with "ne b. na."—"Off and on," "over and under," remind us of 'sub' and 'super.' † Dwollic, MS.

swilce þurh ꝼét into helle pice; Maneʒa ꝼind þa ʒatu. ac heoꞃa nan ne mæiʒ onʒean þæꞃe halʒan ʒelaðunʒe. þe iſ ʒetimbꞃod uppon þam ꝼæſtan ſtane. Cꞃiſte. ꝼoꞃþan ðe se ʒelyꝼeda. þuꞃh Cꞃiſteſ ʒeꞃcýldnýſſe. ætpint þam ꝼꞃeceðnýſſum þæꞃa deoꝼlicꞃa coſtnunʒa;

Ꝥe cpæð. Ic þe betæce heoꝼonan ꞃiceſ cæʒe; Niſ ſeo cæiʒ ʒýlden. ne ſýlꝼꞃen. ne oꝼ nanum antimbꞃe ʒeſmiðod. ac iſ ſe anpealð þe him Cꞃiſt ꝼoꞃʒeaꝼ. þæt nan man ne cýmþ into Godeſ ꞃice. buton ſe halʒa Petꞃuſ him ʒeopeniʒe þæt inꝼæꞃ;

Ǽnd ſpa hpæt ſpa þu bintſt oꝼeꞃ eoꞃðan. þæt bið ʒebunden on heoꝼonum. and ſpa hpæt ſpa ðu unbintſt oꝼeꞃ eoꞃðan. þæt bið unbunden on heoꝼonan;

Ðiſne anpealð he ꝼoꞃʒeaꝼ nu Petꞃe. and eac ſýððan. æꞃ hiſ upſtiʒe. eallum

as it were through a gate into hell's torment. Many are those gates; but none of them shall have power against the holy convocation, which is built upon the firm rock, Christ; because the believer, through Christ's protection, escapes the perils of the devilish temptations.

He said, " I betake* to thee the key of heaven's kingdom." This key is not golden, nor silvren, nor forged of any matter; but is the power which Christ gave him, that no man shall come into God's kingdom, unless the holy Peter open to him the entrance.

"And whatsoever thou shalt bind upon earth, that shall be bound in heaven: and whatsoever thou shalt unbind upon earth, that shall be unbound in heaven."

This power he gave now to Peter; and also afterwards, before his ascension, to

* This word has lost but little of its meaning.

all his apostles, when he breathed on them, thus saying, " Receive the Holy Ghost: the men's sins which ye forgive, shall be forgiven; and from whom ye withhold forgiveness, from them shall forgiveness be withdrawn."

The apostles will not bind any righteous man with their excommunication, nor, through compassion, unbind the wicked man, unless he, with true repentance*, turn to the way of life.

The same power hath the Almighty granted to bishops and holy mass-priests, if they carefully hold it after the evangelical constitution. And therefore is the key specially committed to Peter, that all the community may clearly discern, that whosoever departs from the oneness†

---

* Deed-boot would have been the modern form of the Saxon, *i.e.* amendment of deeds.

† There was oneness [or unity] both in his faith and in his confession; for they are comprised in one book, one chapter, one verse, and one clause of that verse.

hiſ apoſtolum. þa ða he him on aſende.
þus cpeðenðe. Onfoð haliȝne Gaſt;
þæpa manna ſynna þe ȝe foɼȝiſað. beoð
foɼȝyſene. and þam ðe ȝe foɼȝyſe-
nysse oſunnon. him bið oſtoȝen ſeo
foɼȝyſenys*;

Nellað þa apostoli nænne ɲihtpiſne
mið heoɲa manſumunȝe ȝebindan. ne
eac þone manfullan miltſiende unbind-
an. buton he mið ſoþɲe dædbote ȝe-
cyɲɲe to liſeſ peȝe;

Ðone ylcan anpealð hæſð ſe Ælmih-
tiȝa ȝetiðoð biſcopum and halȝum
mæsse-pɲeoſtum. ȝiſ hi hit æſteɲ þæɲe
ȝodſpellican ȝeſetnysse canſullice
healdað; Ac foɲþi iſ ſeo cæȝ Petɲe
ſyndeɲlice betæht. þæt eall þeodſcipe
ȝleaplice tocnape. þæt ſpa hpa ſpa oð-
ſcyt ſɲam annyſſe þæſ ȝeleaſan þe Pe-

* Forgyfenyss, MS. Reg. ut et infra, 102, 3, for-
gyfenyſſ, Cott. Vit. C. V. In both, s for ſ is of fre-
quent occurrence.

ᚱᛁ ıſ þa andette Cꞃıſte. þæt him ne
bıð ᵹetıþod naþoꞃ ne ſynna ꞅoꞃᵹyꞅe-
nſꞅ. ne ınꞅæꞃ þæs heoꞅonlıcan ꞃıces :·
ÆLFRIC: Passio Apostolorum Petri et
Pauli. Ad fid. Cod. MS^ti. Reg. 7.
C. xii. in Mus. Brit.

Qua lingua quove loco precandum sit.

Man mot hıne ᵹebıddan ſpa ſpa he
mæᵹ and can. mıd ælcum ᵹeꞃeoꞃde.
and on ælceꞃe ſtope. Nu ıſ heꞃ on
Enᵹlıſc andetnyſ and ᵹebed : ac ſe þe
þıſ ſınᵹan ꝥylle. ne ꞃecᵹe he na maꞃe
on þæꞃe andetnyſſe þonne he þyꞃcende
þæſ; ꞅoꞃþon þe uꞃe Hælend nele þæt
man on hınc ſylꞅne leoᵹe. ne eac ealle
menn on ane ꞃıſan ne ſynᵹıað :·—
Tib. A. iii.

Ex quodam Lupi Sermone, Ad populum.

Leoꞅan men. undeꞃſtandað þæt

of the faith which Peter then confessed to Christ, to him shall be granted neither forgiveness of sins, nor entrance of the heavenly kingdom.—*Editor's Translation.* See Ælfric Soc. Hom. vol. i. No. 4. p. 368.

In what language or place we ought to pray.

A man may pray according to his ability and knowledge, with every language, and in every place. Now here is a confession and a prayer in English: but whoever will sing this, let him say no more in the confession, than he has [actually] committed; for our Saviour will not have a man lie on himself: either do all men sin in one wise.

From one of Wulfstane's Homilies, To the people.

Beloved men, understand that, in the

first place, every christian man has of all things most need, that he be able to understand God's right, through lore [doctrine] and law.

Of earth were created at first those whom we are come of; and to earth we shall all be turned; and then have either eternal torment aye without end, or eternal bliss, whethersoever we in life have previously earned*.

But let us endeavour, as we have much need, to have a firm faith and full hope in our Lord. And whoever cannot understand right belief through Latin lore, let him learn at least in English, and say thus often, "We believe in one God, Father, Son, and Holy Ghost," &c.

* Note by H. Wanley: Some one has written on the margin, "Here Archbishop Wulfstane clear:

æpept cpiptenpa manna gehpic ah ealpa þinga mæpte þeappe. þæt he cunne Godep piht ongytan. þuph lape and lage;—Ex MS. Bodl.

Op eopðan puþdon gepophte æpept þa ðe pe op comon. and to eopðan pe pculon ealle gepupðan. and pyððan habban þpa ece pite aa buton ende. þpa ece bliþþe. þpa hpæðep þpa pe on lipe æp geeapnodon*;—Ex MS. C. C. C. Cantab. S. 18.

Ac utan don. þpa up mýcel þeapp iþ. habban anpædne geleapan and pulne hiht on upne Dpihten; And þe ðe þuph Leden lape pihtne geleapan undepgýtan ne cunne. geleopnige hupu on Engliþc. and cpeðe þuþ gelome. Credimus in unum Deum, Patrem, Filium, et Spiritum Sanctum, seq^s.—Bibl. Bodl. Jun. 99.

denies a third place after this life." Catalogue, p. 138, col. 1. * Scripsit aliquis in margine, &c.

NOTES TO THE PASCHAL SERMON.

Abbreviations:—J., Joscelyn; L'I., L'Isle; G., W. Guild; R., Ratramnus.

Page. line.

3, 1. *Literally* most beloved, dearest.

    9 & 11. thys *and* that (p. 4, *last line*), *also* those (p. 11, l. 13), *might have been reduced the, as has been done in many places.*

5, 3. Rode tacn, *literally* crucis signum, *needed not to be joined as* rod-treow.

    15. on hande, *J.*; on handa, *as MS., seems better.*

7, 11. that, &c.; with their possessions; *J., L'I., G.*

8, 20. Christ, &c. *should rather be* Jesus Christ. *The Saxon uses* Hælend *for* Jesus, *even where the speaker does not believe that Jesus was the Healer, the Saviour; as in the Gospels,* 'Is not this Jesus the son of Joseph?' *and in the inscription upon the cross.*

12, 1 & 5. as—'at,' *J.*; *and for* with them *read* as their Easter, *so,* as our.

    9. Housell, A.-S. husl, Goth. HUNSI, *a sacrifice, that is a thank-offering, and*

Page. line.

   commemoration of the one great sacrifice,—Gratiarum actio et commemoratio, &c. Fulgentius 'de Fide,'—*quoted and expounded by Ratramnus,* § 90.—*Our Saviour's words, here quoted by our author, could have no reference to the sacrament; and would be equally true though that ordinance had never been instituted.*

15, 11. their successoures, *sic ad literam*, G.; *nec prævideram*; since their departure, J.

  15. Gehwilc *usually means* every; *but here must be* several *or* some; nonnulli, Wheloc—*not translated,* J., L'I.

16, 9. and so forth; and a mountayne, J., L'I., G.; *literally,* and however else.

19, 5. *Mr. Guild has taken an unwarrantable liberty here,*—And they be so truely after the hallowing: But Christ's body, &c.

  8. baptized, christened, J.; *but the word is not* gecristnod, *but* gefullod, *fulled, cleansed, purified. So to baptize is in Icelandic,* skyra, *to scour, clean, brighten,* &c.; brycht and schire, Ja. I. Sc.—Cristnian *is* catechizare (*A*

fred's Bede, 2, 14), *to cat-chize, instruct, make christian, prepare the catechumen for baptism.*

19, 11. Font-vat. *So it is exactly in the Saxon;* font-stone, J.; *the material of which the vessel is formed, is of no moment.*

20, 3. *Better* a corruptible liquor, humor corruptibilis, R. 18.

4. halowing mighte, J.; wholesome virtue, G.; virtus sanabilis, R.

23, 6. Lyving, enlivened; Rationalis animæ spiritu vivificata (caro), R.

24, 13. Some chewe lesse deale, J.; some chewe the lesse, G. *Without grammar or dictionary, the Saxonists of that day had often to grope their way in the dark. The indecorous* chewe *has no foundation in the Saxon:* gesceotan, *to be allotted, remains stereotyped in the phrase,* scot and lot: menn, *here, as often elsewhere, was taken for the nom. pl.;* sume, *supposed or made to agree with it* (MSS. sumum); gesceote, *as a plural, could stand only before a personal pronoun;*

Page. line.

  and læsse dæl *is not, as appears to have been assumed, an acc. neut., but* læssa dæl, *nom. s. m. as in MSS.; though to some* [one] *man be allotted a less dole, share, or portion, &c.*

25, 18. Wedd and hiw, Pignus et species, *R.* 88; *also* Pignus et Imago, 86.

26, 3 & 4. We .... urum, *MS.*

  6. on oþære, *J.*—7. uitas, *J.*; 27, 7. *uita, J., so MS., otherwise,* uitæ.

27, 14. brake, *Sax.* to-brake, *or* to-broke; *so,* "all to-brake," *Judges* ix. 53; completely broke asunder, *often falsely printed* to break; *so,* 15, "deuided;" *S.* to-lithed, *dismembered,* lith and limb, *a common phrase in Sc.*

31, 6 & 7. "They received, who believed," *G., and so it is in the original.*

32, 5. for, or as a man,—to men, *J.*—to be a man, *G.*

35, 8. encompassed,—invested, *Thorpe;*—going about, *J.*;—in which he was apprehended, *Editor of Ratr.* 1688, p. 332, *Note; not aware that he quoted at p.* 379, *Note, the very words which*

Page.	line.	
		Ælfric had translated, carnem qua indutum erat Verbum, *Aug. in Joh. Tr.* 27.
39,	3.	To that whiche,—"whiche misterye," *J.*, "for that which," *Thorpe. Our author appears not to have taken a full view of the context* : Mysterium vestrum in mensa Domini positum est. Mysterium vestrum accipitis, ad id quod estis "Amen" respondetis, et respondendo subscribitis. Audis ergo "Corpus Christi," et respondes "Amen:" esto membrum Christi, ut verum sit "Amen." *Aug. ap. Ratr.* 95. *Ælfric's* to þam ðe *may be rendered* as that which; *Augustine's Latin* to that whiche ye are ye answer Amen.
40,	4.	ungyltynes and innocencye of harte. To an, &c., *J. So G., inserting the omitted clause,* if they be not oppressed with sinne.
43,	7.	on thys day, *that is, on the day which this represents or commemorates. From such usual modes of expression* **Ratramn.** *(after Augustine) elegantly*

Page. line.

argues that this is my body.... broken, &c. *signifies*, this represents and commemorates the body of our Lord, broken for us; *R.* 35–38.

44, 10. shall, *J.*
47, 8. did burne.—9. brake not, *J.*
48, 18. cover and wrap in that c., *G.*
50, 10 & 11. hy cáflice æton, *MS., the true reading,—interlined* sceoldon *in the handwriting of Joscelin as is supposed, with* æton *untouched.*
51, 7. best, *or* better; *but instead of* bet *in the A.-S. the MS. reads* béc, who know books, and have ability; *perhaps right.*
    14. quicknes and hast, *J.*; and hastiness, *G.*
52, 4. wounde, *G.*; hange, *J.*
57, 4. Wulfsine; Wulfine, *J.*
    14. Be preost sinoþe, that is, a Synode concerning priestes, *J.* Be preoste synoðe, *MSS.*; *but,* Be preost-synoðe *must be the true reading.*—De Synodo Sacerdotali, *MS. H.* 438.
58, 3 & 13. sceocum, *J.*
    9. mus (p. 59, mouse), *J.*
61, 1. gebletsode.—3. halgan (holye), *J.*

Page. line.

64, 4. vpon.—7. on, *J.*, *for* in.
66, 1. *read* gelic.
67, 1. those heretikes who do, *J.*
69, 18. gastlicum, *J.*
71, 7. mistery,..... they, *J.*
72, 15. thy excellencie, *properly* your hollness.
79, 20. cristendome, *J. & H.* 441; cristendom, 438; gehalden, *J.*, gehealden, 441,— gehealdan, 438; *better* gehealdon, *with MS. point after* geleafan.
80, 18. geleafan and, *J. and Nero,* A. I.—20. oþrum, *J.*; þam oþrum, *MS. But the reading adopted has been subsequently found in a homily of Wulfstane; Wheloc's Bede,* p. 486.
83, 14. to hym, *J.*
89, 9. ye, *J., but* eow *is* you, to *or* for you, *or* yourselves.—17. he, *J.*, rested him, *S.*
93, 17. *End of Joscelyn's Work. An explanation of the Saxon characters is added.*
97, 13. *The reading adopted has been since observed, as given from a Cambridge MS. in Wheloc's Notes,* p. 238.—*Also* dwollic.
100, 16. all the, *perhaps* every; omnis natio, *Wheloc.*

THE OFFICES

OF

THE CANONICAL HOURS:

A BENEDICTINE LITURGY OF THE TENTH CENTURY,

IN LATIN AND ANGLO-SAXON.

COLLATED WITH ANCIENT MANUSCRIPTS, AND TRANSLATED INTO MODERN ENGLISH.

De Officiis diurnalium et nocturnalium horarum.

GODCUND ðeowdom is gesett on cyriclicum þenungum æfter canoneclican gewunan to nyd-rihte eallum gehadedum mannum. On ælcne timan man sceal God herian, and on ælcere stowe georne to Gode clypian. Ac þeah-hwæðere syndon gesette timan synderlice to þam anum, þæt gyf hwa for bysgan oftor ne mæge, þæt he huru þæt nyd-riht dæghwamlice gefille; eallswa Dauid cwæð: Septies in die laudem dixi tibi: þæt is, Seofon siðon on dæg ic sang ðe, Drihten, to lofe and to weorðunge.

To seldan hit bið, beo hit a-seldor on dæg, þæt we God herian, þonne seofon siðum; þæt is, ænne ærest on ærne morgen, and eft on undern-tide, and on midne dæg, and on non, and on æfen,

Of the Offices of the daily and nightly hours.

DIVINE service is appointed in ecclesiastical ministrations according to canonical usages as a necessary duty to all ordained men. At every time we ought to praise God, and in every place heartily to call upon God. But nevertheless there are set times especially for that alone, that if any [one] on account of business may not oftener, he may at least daily fulfill the necessary duty; as David says: Septies in die laudem dixi tibi; that is, Seven times a-day, Lord, 1 sang to thy praise and worship.

Too seldom it is, if it be seldomer a-day, that we praise God, than seven times; that is, once first at early morn, and again at the third hour, and at midday, and at noon, and at even, and at fore-night, and at midnight. (? Cock-crowing.)

It never is any man's capacity that he can praise God so much as He is worthy. But yet it is incumbent upon us all, that we heartily serve and worship him as far as we may and can.

Of the morning office. (*Matins.*)

At day-break we ought to praise God, as David says: Deus, Deus meus, ad te de luce vigilo: That is, My Lord, to thee I wake from the dawn. And again he says, In matutinis, Domine, meditabor in te; quia fuisti adjutor meus: That is, At day-break I will meditate on thee, because thou wert my help. Christ is the help of all mankind, and the preserver of the whole world.

At day-break it was, that Moses, by the power of God, led the people of Israel out of the land of Egypt, all unharmed, over the red sea. And after

and on foran-niht, and on uhtan timan.

Nis æfre æniges mannes mæð þæt he cunne God swa forð geherian swa he wyrðe is. Ac hit is þeah ure ealra þearf, þæt we geornlice him þeowian and ðenian þæs ðe we magon and cunnon.

De matutinali officio. (*Dægred-sang.*)

On dægred man sceal God herian, eall-swa Dauid cwæð: Deus, Deus meus, ad te de luce vigilo: Ðæt is, Min Drihten, to þe ic wacige of frum-leohte. And eft he cwæð: In matutinis, Domine, meditabor in te; quia fuisti adjutor meus: Ðæt is, On dægred ic smeage ymbe þe; forðam þe ðu wære min fultum. Crist is ealles mancynnes fultum, and ealles middan-eardes helpend.

On dægred hit gewearð þæt þurh Godes mihte Moyses gelædde þæt Israhelitisce folc of Egipta lande, ealle unwemme, ofer ða readan sæ. And æfter ðam sona seo sylfe sæ besencte and adrencte Godes wiðerwinnan, Pharaonem and ealle his gegenge. And on dægred hit gewearð þæt Crist of deaþe aras, and of helle gelædde ealle ða ðe he wolde; and his wiðerwinnan, þæt is, deofol sylfne he besencte, and ealle his gegenge, on helle susle. Þy we sculon on dægred God georne herian, and him á þancian ðære mildheortnysse þe he on mancynne þa geworhte, þa þa he hit alysde of helle wite, and of deofles gewealde, and gerymde þanon forð rihtne weg to heofona rice ælcum þara þe his willan gewyrcð her on life. Amen.

De prima hora. (*Prim-sang.*)

On þære forman dæg-tide, þæt is, be sunnan up-gange, we sculon God herian, and hine geornlice biddan, þæt he þurh his mildheortnysse, mid soþre

that immediately the same sea overwhelmed and drowned God's adversaries, Pharaoh and all his company. And at day-break it was, that Christ arose from death, and led from hell all those whom he would, and overwhelmed his adversaries, that is, the devil himself, and all his company, in hell's torments. Therefore we ought at day-break willingly to praise God, and ever to thank him for the mercy which he then wrought on mankind, when he delivered them from the punishment of hell, and from the power of the devil; and opened thenceforth a straight way to the kingdom of heaven for every one who works his will here in life. Amen.

Of the first hour. (*Prime.*)

At the first hour of the day, that is, about sun-rise, we ought to praise God, and earnestly to pray him, that he through his mercy may enlighten our hearts with the light of the true sun; that is, that he by his grace may enlighten our minds, that the devil may not be able by pernicious darkness to lead us astray from the right way, nor to impede us too much with the snares of sin.

God, attend for my help, hasten to help me.—[Ps. lxx. 1.]

>Be, Lord God,
>a precious aid,
>behold me, Lord
>and quickly then
>help me
>at extreme need.

GLORY TO THE FATHER.

To thee be glory and praise
widely extended
through all nations,
favour and will,
might and mercy,
and every mind's love,

sunnan lihtincge, ure heortan alihte;
þæt is, þæt he þurh his gyfe ure inge-
þance swa alihte, þæt us deofol of rihtan
wege þurh deriende ðystra belædan ne
mæge, ne mid syn-grinum to swyðe
gehremman.

Deus in adiutorium meum intende
ad adiuuandum me festina.
    Wes. Drihten God,
      œore fullum;
      beheald, Drihten, me,
      and me hraðe syððan
      gefultuma
      æt feorh-þearfe.

GLORIA PATRI.

Sy þe wuldor and lof
wide geopenod
geond ealle þeoda,
þanc and willa,
mægen and mildse,
and ealles modes lufu,

soðfæstra sib,
and ðines sylfes dom
worulde gewlitegod;
swa ðu wealdan miht
eall eorðan mægen,
and up-lyfte,
wind and wolcna;
wealdest ealle on riht.

PATRI ET FILIO ET SPIRITUI SANCTO.

Þu eart frofra Fæder
and feorh-hyrde,
lifes latteow,
leohtes wealdend,
asyndrod fram synnum;
swa ðin Sunu mære,
þurh clæne gecynd
Cyning ofer ealle,
bealde gebletsod;
boca Lareow,
heah hige-frofre,
and Halig Gast:

peace of the faithful,
and thy own judgement
to the world manifested;
how thou canst govern
every power of earth,
and the lofty sky,
wind and clouds;
rulest all in right.

To the Father and to the Son and to the Holy Ghost.

Thou art the Father of comforts
and the Guardian [and]
Guide of life,
Ruler of light,
separate from sins;
so thy glorious Son,
by pure nature
King over all,
greatly blessed;
Teacher of the Scriptures,
high comfort of mind,
and Holy Ghost.

As it was in the beginning.

As was in the beginning
the Lord of mankind,
of all the world
the beauty and comfort,
pure and powerful.
Thou shewedst that
when thou, eternal God,
alone createdst
by holy might
heavens and earth,
the lands and lofty sky
and every thing.
Thou settest on earth
very many kinds
and severedst them
afterwards in multitude.
Thou createdst, eternal God,
all creatures
in six days,
and on the seventh thou restedst.
Then was completed
thy fair work ;
and thou Sunday

Sicut erat in principio.

Swa wæs on fruman
Frea mancynnes,
ealre worulde
wlite and frofer,
clæne and cræftig.
Þu gecyddest þæt
ða ðu, ece God,
ana geworhtest
þurh halige miht
heofonas and eorðan,
eardas and up-lyft,
and ealle þing.
Ðu settest on foldan
swyðe feala cynna
and tosyndrodost hig
syððan on mænego.
Þu geworhtest, ece God,
ealle gesceafta,
on six dagum,
and on þone seofoðan þu gerestest.
Ða wæs geforðad
þin fægere weorc;
and þu sunnandæg

sylf halgodest,
and gemærsodest hine
manegum to helpe.
Ðone heahan dæg
healdað and freoðiað
ealle þa ðe cunnon
cristene þeawas,
halige heort-lufan,
and ðæs Hehstan gebod:
on Drihtnes naman
se dæg is gewurðod.

ET NUNC ET SEMPER.

And nu and symble
þine soðan weorc,
and ðin mycele miht,
manegum swutelað;
swa þinc cræftas
heo cyðað wide
ofer ealle woruld.
Ece standeð
Godes hand-geweorc,
groweð swa ðu hete.
Ealle þe heriað

thyself hallowedst,
and magnifiedst it
for a help to many.
The high day
hold and observe
all who know
christian manners,
holy heart-love,
and the Highest's command:
in the Lord's name
the day is honoured.

BOTH NOW AND EVER.

And now and always
thy true works,
and thy great might
to many are manifest;
as thy powers
shew themselves widely
over all the world.
Eternal standeth
God's hand-iwork,
groweth as thou badest.
All holy joys

praise thee
with a pure voice,
and christian books,
all the mid-region;
and we men say
on the ground here
to God praise and thank,
eternal will, (*or* delight,)
and thy own judgement.

AND TO AGES OF AGES*.

And to worlds of worlds
shall dwell and reign
the King in glory;
and his chosen [ones]
high majesties,
holy spirits,
beauteous angels;
and glorious grace,
true peace,
thanking of souls,
mercy of mind.
There is the greatest love,

* Or, "world [*i. e.* ages] without end."

halige dreamas
clænre stefne,
and cristene bec,
eall middan-eard;
and we men cweðað
on grunde her
Gode lof and ðanc,
ece willa,
and ðin agen dom.

ET IN SECULA SECULORUM.

And on worulda woruld
wunað and rixað
Cyning innan wuldre;
and his þa gecorenan
heah-þrymnesse,
halige gastas,
wlitige englas,
and wuldor-gyfe,
soðe sibbe,
sawla þangung*,
modes miltse.
Ðær is seo mæste lufu,

* þancung, Cod. MS. C. C. C. Cantab.

halige domas.
Heofonas syndon
þurh þine ecan 'word'*
æghwær fulle.
Swa syndon þine mihta
ofer middan-geard
swutele and gesyne,
þæt ðu hy sylf worhtest.

AMEN.

We þæt soðlice
secgað ealle.
Þurh clæne gecynd
þu eart cyning on riht,
clæne and cræftig;
þu gecyddest þæt,
ða þu, mihtig God,
man geworhtest,
and him on dydest
oruð and sawul;
sealdest word and gewitt,
and wæstma gecynd;
cyddest þine cræftas:
Swylc is Cristes miht.

* From the same MS.—not in MS. Bodl.

holy judgements.
The heavens are
through thy eternal words
everywhere full.
Thus are thy powers
over the mid-region
manifest and seen,
that thou thyself wroughtest them.

TRUELY.

We that " TRUELY "
say all.
Through pure nature
thou art King in right
pure and powerful :
thou shewedst that,
when thou, mighty God,
createdst man,
and in him puttest
breath and soul ;
gavest word and wit,
and nature of increase ;
shewedst thy powers :
Such is Christ's might.

HYMN.

Now, the star of day arisen,
Let us humbly pray to God.

God, save me in thy name; and deliver me in thy might.

In thy holy name
save me, O God;
free me from enemies
through thy dear power.

And to the King of ages, immortal, invisible, the only God, [be] honour and glory for ever. Amen.

Thanks to God.

Christ Jesus, Son of the living God, with the Holy Spirit, have mercy upon us.

Who sittest at the right hand of the Father, have mercy on us.

Glory to the Father.

Christ Jesus!—Arise, Lord, help us for thy name's sake.

Arise, Lord, now,

HYMNUS.

Iam lucis orto sidere
Deum precemur supplices.

Deus in nomine tuo saluum me fac;
et in uirtute tua libera me.

On þinum þam halgan naman
gedo me halne, God;
alys me fram laðum
þurh þin leofe mægen.

Regi autem seculorum immortali invisibili soli Deo honor et gloria in secula seculorum. Amen.

Deo gratias.

Christe Iesu, fili Dei uiui, cum Sancto Spiritu, miserere nobis.

Qui sedes ad dextram Patris miserere nobis.

Gloria Patri.

Christe Iesu. Exsurge Domine, adiuua nos propter nomen tuum.

Aris Drihten nu,

and us ricene do
fælne fultum,
and us æt feondum ahredde;
forðon we naman þinne
nyde lufiað.
 Cyrie leison.
 Christe leison.
 Cyrie leison.

PATER NOSTER QUI ES IN CELIS,
&c.

Fæder mancynnes,
frofres ic þe bidde,
halig Drihten,
þu þe on heofonum eart;
þæt sy gehalgod
hyge-cræftum fæst
þin nama nu ða,
neriende Crist,
in urum ferhð-locan,
fæste gestaðelod.
Cume nu to mannum,
mihta Wealdend,
þin rice to us,

and to us quickly make
kindly aid,
and rid us from foes;
for we thy name
intensely love.
    Lord pity us.
    Christ pity us.
    Lord pity us.

OUR FATHER WHO ART IN HEAVEN, &c.

Father of mankind,
of comfort I thee pray,
holy Lord,
thou who art in heaven;
that be hallowed
in the mind's powers fast
thy name even now,
Saviour Christ,
in our mind's recess
firmly established.
Come now to men,
Lord of mights,
thy kingdom, [even] to us,

righteous Judge,
and thy belief,
in our life-day,
within our mind
gloriously dwell.
And thy will with us
be performed
in the habitation
of earth's kingdom,
as it purely is
in heaven's glory
with joys celebrated
aye to ages forth.
Give us to-day,
Lord of men,
High King of heaven,
our bread,
which thou sendest
on the earth,
for health to souls
of the race of men ;
that is the pure
Christ the Lord God.
Forgive us, Guardian of men,

rihtwis Dema,
and ðin geleafa,
in lif-dæge,
on urum mode
mære þurhwunige.
And þin willa mid us
weorðe gelæsted
on eardunge
eorðan rices,
swa hluttor is
in heofon-wuldre
wynnum gewlitegod
á to woruld forð.
Syle us to-dæge,
Drihten gumena,
heofena heah Cyning,
hlaf urne, (userne)
þone þu onsendest
sawlum to hæle,
on middan-eard,
manna cynnes;
þæt is se clæna
Crist Drihten God.
Forgif us, gumena Weard,

gyltas and synna,
and ure leahtras alet,
lices wunda,
and mún-dæda;
swa we mildum wið ðe
ælmihtigum Gode
oft abylgeað;
swa swa we forlætað
leahtras on corþan
þam þe wið us
oft agyltað,
and him wom-dæde
witan ne þencað,
for earnunge
ecan lifes.
Ne læd þu us to wite
in wean sorge,
ne in costnunge,
Crist nerigende;
þylæs we arlease
ealra þinra mildsa
þurh feondscipe
fremde weorðan.
And wið yfele gefreo us

[our] guilts and sins,
and our vices remit,
the body's wounds,
and evil deeds;
as we against thee, [the] merciful
almighty God,
often offend;
so as we forgive
faults on earth
to those who against us
often trespass,
and them for evil deeds
think not to blame,
for the obtaining
of eternal life.
Lead thou us not for torment
into woe's sorrow,
nor into temptation,
Christ the Saviour;
lest we impious
to all thy mercies,
through enmity,
become strangers.
And from evil free us

also even now
of every foe.
We in our inmost soul,
King of angels,
thanks and glory,
true Lord of victory,
heartily express:
because thou mercifully
by might redeemedst us
from the bondage
of hell's torment.
  So be it.

My soul shall live, and shall praise thee, and thy judgements shall help me.

My soul shall live,
and thee gladly praise,
and me thy judgements
indeed shall help.

I erred as a sheep which had been lost; seek thy servant, Lord, for I have not forgotten thy commandments.

I strayed as
the foolish sheep,

eac nu ða
feonda gehwylces.
We in ferhð-locan,
Ðeoden engla,
þanc and wuldor,
soð sige-drihten,
secgað georne ;
þæs þe þu us milde
mihtum alysdest
fram hæft-nyde
helle wites.
 Weorðe þæt.

Viuet anima mea et laudabit te, et iudicia tua adiuuabunt me

Leofað sawul min,
and þe lustum hereð,
and me þine domas
dædum fultumiað.

Erraui sicut ouis quæ perierat; require seruum tuum Domine, quia mandata tua non sum oblitus.

Ic gedwelede swa
þæt dysige sceap,

þæt þe forwurðan
wolde, huru la
sec þinne esne
elne, Drihten,
forðon ic þinra beboda
ne forgeat beorhtra æfre.

CREDO IN DEUM PATREM OMNI-POTENTEM, &c.

Ælmihtig Fæder
up on rodore,
þe ða sciran gesceaft
sceope and worhtest,
and eorðan wang
ealne gesettest;
ic þe, ecne God
ænne gecenne,
lustum gelyfe.
Þu eart lifes Frea,
engla ordfruma,
eorðan wealdend;
and þu garsecges
grundas geworhtest;
and þu ða manego canst

which perish
would; at least O
seek thy servant
with fervour, Lord,
for thy bright commandments
I never forgot.

I BELIEVE IN GOD THE FATHER ALMIGHTY, ET CETERA.

Almighty Father
up in the sky,
who the bright creation
shapedst and wroughtest,
and earth's plain
all settest:
I thee one eternal
God acknowledge,
[and] gladly believe.
Thou art life's Lord,
prime origin of angels,
earth's Ruler,
and thou the ocean's
depths createdst;
and thou the multitude knowest

of the glorious stars.
I on thy true
Son believe,
the saving King,
hither sent
from the lofty
realm of angels;
whom Gabriel,
God's messenger,
to the holy Mary
herself announced:
A woman immaculate!
She the message
received nobly,
and thee [her] Father's self
under the inclosure of her breast
[as] a child conceived.
There was not perpetrated
a crime at the espousals;
but there the Holy Ghost
the earnest gave,
the virgin's bosom
filled with bliss;
and she certainly

mærra tungla.
Ic on Sunu þinne
soðne gelyfe,
hælendne Cyning,
hider asendne
of þam uplican
engla rice;
þone Gabriel,
Godes ærend-raca,
sancta Marian
sylfre gebodode,
ides unmæne.
Heo þæt ærende
onfeng freolice,
and ðe Fæder sylfne
under breost-locan
bearn acende.
Næs þær gefremmed
firen æt giftum;
ac þær Halig Gast
hand-gyft sealde,
þære fæmnan bosm
fylde mid blisse;
and heo cuðlice

cende swa mærne
eorð-buendum
engla Scyppend;
se to frofre gewearð
fold-buendum;
and ymbe Bethleem
bodedon englas,
þæt acenned wæs
Crist on eorðan.
Þa se Pontisca
Pilatus weold
under Romwarum
rices and doma,
þa se deora Frea
deað þrowade,
on galgan astah,
gumena Drihten:
þone geomor-mod
Iosep byrigde;
and he of helle
huðe gefette,
of þam susl-hofe,
sawla manega;
het ða uplican

to earth's inhabitants
thus bore the glorious
Creator of angels;
who was for consolation
to the dwellers on the ground;
and about Bethlehem
angels proclaimed
that born was
Christ on earth.
Then the Pontish
Pilate ruled
under the Romans
the kingdom and judgements,
when the dear Lord
suffered death,
on the gallows mounted,
the Lord of men:
whom, sorrowful in mind
Joseph buried;
and he from hell
the booty fetched
of many souls,
from the abode of torment,
[and] bade them the lofty

country seek.
Therefore on the third day
the Ruler of peoples
arose, the kingdom's Lord,
speedily from the dust.
And he forty days
his followers
with counsels cheered,
and then began
to seek his kingdom,
the lofty country.
He said that he would
none forsake,
who forth beyond that
would follow him,
and with firm mind
shew goodwill.
I with hope embrace
the Holy Ghost,
equally eternal as is
either called
Father or noble Son
in peoples' languages.
Not are these three Gods,

eþel secan.
Þæs þy ðriddan dæge
þeoda Wealdend
aras, rices Frea,
recene of moldum.
And he feowertig daga
folgeras sine
runum arette;
and ða his rice began
þone uplican
eðel secan.
Cwæð þæt he nolde
nænne forlætan,
þe him forð ofer þæt
filian wolde,
and mid fæstum sefan
freode gelæstan.
Ic Haligne Gast
hihte beluce,
emne swa ecne swa is
aðor gecweden,
Fæder oððe freo Bearn
folca gereordum.
Ne synd þæt þreo Godas,

þriwa genemned;
ac is an God,
se ðe ealle hafað
þa þry naman
þinga gerynum,
soð and sige-fæst,
ofer side gesceaft,
wereda wuldor-gyfa,
wlanc and ece.
Eac ic gelyfe,
þæt syn leofe Gode*,
þe þurh ænne geþanc
Ealdor heriað,
heofona heah-cyning,
her for life.
And ic gemænscipe

* Dr. Hickes has given a singular version of this line:—
    That Spouse beloved of God,
    The Holy Church:

in a marginal Note he supports his view by quoting a number of texts in which the Church is designated the Spouse. But the whole of his version and his Note are founded upon the word 'syn,' which he took for a noun signifying 'spouse,' upon what authority does not appear; whereas it is merely the substantive verb used elliptically for þa syn, they or those

[though] thrice named;
but is one God,
who hath all
those three names
by mysteries of things,
true and triumphant,
over the wide creation,
the glory-giver of hosts,
lofty and eternal.
Also I believe
that [they] are dear to God
who through one thought
praise the Lord,
heaven's high King,
here for life.
And I believe

are, as more fully expressed by Lupus or Wulfstane in his Sermo de Fide Catholica,—a paraphrase of the Creed:—

Leofan men, we gelyfað þæt halige gelaþung sy ealra cristenra manna to anum rihtan geleafan, and þæt þa syn Gode leofe þe þurh anfeald geþanc hine lufiað and heriað. Wheloc's Bede, p. 488.

Beloved men, we believe that there is a holy convocation of all christian men to one right faith, and that those are dear to God who by simple thought [single-mindedness] love and praise him.

the grand communion
of thy saints
here for life.
Remission I believe
of every crime.
And I the resurrection
believe of all men's
flesh on earth,
at the dreadful hour.
There thou eternal life
to all wilt deal,
as here every man
shall please the Creator.

And I have cried to thee, O Lord, and in the morning my prayer shall prevent thee.

I now to thee,
eternal Lord,
with earnest thought
have mightily cried;
and my prayer
every morning
before thyself
sincere shall come.

mærne getreowe
þinra haligra
her for life.
Lisse ic gelyfe
leahtra gehwylces.
And ic þone ærist
ealra getreowe
flæsces on foldan,
on þa forhtan tid.
Þær þu ece lif
eallum dælest,
swa her manna gehwylc
Metode gecwemað.

Et ego ad te Domine clamaui; et mane oratio mea preueniet te.

Ic nu to ðe,
ece Drihten,
mid mod-gehygde
mægne clypode;
and min gebed
morgena gehwylce
fore sylfne ðe
soðfæst becume.

Uerba mea auribus percipe Domine;
intellige clamorem meum.

> Word þu min onfoh,
> wuldres Ealdor,
> and mid earum gehyr,
> ece Drihten.

Intende voci orationis meæ, rex meus
et Deus meus.

> Ongyt mine clypunga
> cuðum gereorde;
> beheald min gebed
> holdum mode;
> þu eart min Cyning,
> and eac ece God.

Quoniam ad te orabo Domine; mane
exaudies uocem meam.

> Forðon ic to ðe,
> ece Drihten,
> soðum gebidde;
> and þu symble gehyr
> morgena gehwylce
> mine stefne.

Perceive with [thine] ears my words
O Lord; understand my cry.

> Receive thou my word,
> King of glory,
> and with ears hear,
> eternal Lord.

Attend to the voice of my prayer
my King and my God.

> Understand my crying
> with known speech;
> behold my prayer
> with favourable mind:
> Thou art my King,
> and also eternal God.

For I will pray to thee, Lord; in the morning thou shalt hear my voice.

> For I to thee,
> eternal Lord,
> will truly pray;
> and thou always hear
> every morning
> my voice.

For thou art not a God willing iniquity. In the morning I will stand by thee, and will see.

> I will stand by thee
> early in the morning,
> and to thee [thy]self will look;
> because for a truth I wot
> that thou, Lord, willest not
> any iniquity.

Thy ways, Lord, make known to me, and thy paths teach thou me.

> Make thy ways to me
> intelligible, Lord;
> and teach me also
> the steps of thy paths.

Direct me in thy truth, and teach me; for thou art God my Saviour; and I have waited for thee the whole day.

> Direct me in counsel,
> and speedily teach me,
> that I in thy truth
> may ever live.

Quoniam non Deus uolens iniquitatem tu es. Mane adstabo tibi et videbo.

> Ic þe ætstande
> ær on morgen,
> and ðe sylfne geseo;
> forðon ic to soðe wat,
> þæt ðu unriht ne wilt
> ænig, Drihten.

Uias tuas, Domine, notas fac mihi; et semitas tuas edoce me.

> Do me wegas þine
> wise, Drihten;
> and me ðinra stiga
> stapas eac gelær.

Dirige me in ueritate tua, et doce me; quia tu es Deus salutaris meus, et te sustinui tota die.

> Gerece me on ræde,
> and me ricene gelær,
> þæt ic on þinre soðfæstnysse
> symble lyfige.

Reminiscere miserationum tuarum Domine et misericordiæ tuæ; quæ a seculo sunt.

>Wes þu gemyndig
>miltsa þinra,
>þe ðu, Drihten, dydest
>syððan dagas wæron,
>and ðu wislice
>þas woruld gesettest.

Delicta iuuentutis meæ et ignorantias meas ne memineris Domine; secundum magnam misericordiam tuam memor esto mei.

>Ne gemynega þu me
>minra fyrena
>gramra to georne,
>þe ic geong dyde,
>and me uncuðe
>æghwær wæron:
>For þinre þære myclan
>mildheortnysse
>weorð gemyndig min,
>mihtig Drihten.

Remember thy compassions, Lord, and thy mercy; which are from the age [from everlasting].

> Be thou mindful
> of thy mercies,
> which thou, Lord, didest
> since days were,
> and thou wisely
> this world establishedst.

The faults of my youth, and my ignorances remember not, Lord; according to thy great mercy be mindful of me.

> Remember thou not to me
> my heinous crimes
> too earnestly,
> which I young committed,
> and to me unknown
> were everywhere:
> For thy great
> mercy
> be mindful of me,
> mighty Lord.

Judge, Lord, them that hurt me; defeat them that fight against me.

> Judge, Lord, now
> those who formerly hurt me
> fight likewise against those
> who fought against me.

Lay hold on arms and shield; and arise to my aid.

> Seize spear and shield
> and willingly stand up
> in aid to me
> against the terror of foes.

Discharge the lance, and close against those, who pursue me: say to my soul, I am thy salvation.

> Guard me with war-weapons
> against the unfavourable;
> and with war enclose me
> from cruel foes,
> who are all
> persecuting me:
> say then afterwards

Iudica Domine nocentes me; expugna impugnantes me.

> Dem Drihten nu
> þa me deredon ær,
> afeoht swylce
> þa me fuhtan to.

Apprehende arma et scutum; et exsurge in adiutorium mihi.

> Gegrip gar and scyld
> and me georne gestande
> on fultume
> wið feonda gryre.

Effunde frameam, et conclude aduersus eos, qui me persecuntur: dic anime meæ salus tua ego sum.

> Heald me here-wæpnum
> wið unholdum;
> and wige beluc
> wraðum feondum,
> þe min ehtend
> ealle syndon:
> sæge þonne syððan

sawle minre,
þæt ðu hire on hæle
hold gestode.

Repleatur os meum laude tua, ut possim cantare gloriam tuam.

Sy min muð and min mod
mægne gefylled,
þæt ic þin lof mæge
lustum singan,
and wuldor ðin
wide mærsian,
and ðe ealne dæg
æghwær herian.

Auerte faciem tuam a peccatis meis; et omnes iniquitates meas dele.

Awend þine ansyne
á fram minum
fræcnum fyrenum;
and nu forð heonon
eall min unriht adwæsc
æghwær symle.

to my soul
that thou for her salvation
hast stood favourable.

Let my mouth be filled with thy praise, that I may chant thy glory.

> Be my mouth and my mind
> mightily filled,
> that I thy praise may
> gladly sing,
> and thy glory
> largely magnify,
> and thee all the day
> everywhere praise.

Turn away thy face from my sins; and blot out all my iniquities.

> Turn away thy countenance
> aye from my
> presumptuous crimes;
> and now henceforth
> all my iniquity blot out
> everywhere always.

A clean heart create in me, O God; and a right spirit renew in my bowels.

> Give me, holy God,
> a clean heart;
> and a right spirit,
> God, renew
> in my mind
> especially, my Lord.

Cast me not forth from thy face; and take not thy holy spirit away from me.

> Cast thou me not,
> Lord of glory,
> from thy face
> for evermore;
> especially bear not away
> the holy Ghost,
> that he to me suddenly
> become strange.

Restore to me the joy of thy salvation; and with thy principal spirit confirm me.

> Give me thy salvation's

Cor mundum crea in me Deus; et spiritum rectum innova in uisceribus meis.

> Syle me, halig God,
> heortan clæne;
> and rihtne gast
> God geniwa
> on minre gehigde
> huru, min Drihten.

Ne proiicias me a facie tua; et spiritum sanctum tuum ne auferas a me.

> Ne awyrp þu me,
> wuldres Ealdor,
> fram ðinre ansyne
> æfre to feore;
> ne huru on-weg aber
> þone halgan Gast,
> þæt he me færinga
> fremde wyrðe.

Redde michi lætitiam salutaris tui; et Spiritu principali confirma me.

> Syle me þinre hælu

holde blisse ;
and me ealdorlice
æþele Gaste
on ðinne willan getryme
weroda Drihten.

**Eripe me Domine ab homine malo;
a uiro iniquo libera me.**

Genere me wið niðe,
for naman þinum ;
fram yfelum men,
ece Drihten.

Eripe me de inimicis meis Deus meus; et ab insurgentibus in me libera me.

Ahredde me, halig God,
hefiges niðes
feonda minra,
þe me feohtað to ;
alys me fram laðum,
þe me lungre on
risan willað
nymþe þu me ræd gife.

gracious joy;
and with thy princely
noble Spirit
in thy will confirm me,
Lord of hosts.

Rescue me, Lord, from the evil man;
from the unjust man free me.

Save me from malice,
for thy name;
from an evil man,
eternal Lord.

Rescue me from my enemies, O my God; and from those rising against me deliver me.

Rid me, holy God,
of the heavy malice
of my foes,
that fight against me;
free me from the wicked
who will instantly
rise upon me
unless thou give me counsel.

Rescue me from those who work iniquity; and from the man of blood save me.

> Save me from the malice
> of evil-doers,
> who here unrightly
> all work;
> and me from the blood-thirsty man's
> violence preserve.

So I will sing a psalm to thy name for ever; that I may pay my vows from day to day.

> So I to thy name
> by constraint will sing,
> that I my vow
> may here pay
> from day to day,
> as it is meet.

Hear us, God our Saviour, the Hope of all the ends of the earth, and on the sea afar.

> Hear us saviour God;

Eripe me de operantibus iniquitatem; et de uiro sanguinum salua me.

> Genere me fram niðe
> naht fremmendra,
> þe her unrihtes
> ealle wyrceað;
> and me wið blod-hreowes weres
> bealuwe gehæle.

Sic psalmum dicam nominl tuo in seculum seculi; ut reddam uota mea de die in diem.

> Swa ic naman þinum
> neode singe,
> þæt [ic] min gehat
> her agylde
> of dæge on dæg,
> swa hit gedefe wese.

Exaudi nos Deus salutaris noster, spes omnium finium terre, et in mari longe,

> Gehyr us, hælend God;

þu eart hiht ealra
þe on ðisse eorðan
utan syndon,
oððe feor on sæ
foldum wuniað.

Benedic anima mea, Domino; et omnia interiora mea nomen sanctum eius.

Bletsa mine sawle
bliðe Drihten;
and eall min ineran
his þone ecan naman.

Benedic anima mea Domino; et noli oblivisci omnes retributiones eius.

Bletsige mine sawle
bealde Drihten;
ne wilt ðu ofergeotul
æfre weorðan
ealra goda,
þe he ðe ær dyde.

Qui propitiatur omnibus iniquitatibus tuis; qui sanat omnes languores tuos.

> thou art the hope of all
> who on this earth
> without are,
> or far in the sea
> in lands dwell.

Bless, O my soul, the Lord; and all my inner [parts], bless his holy name.

> Bless, O my soul,
> blithely the Lord;
> and all my inner [parts],
> his eternal name.

Bless, O my soul, the Lord; and will not to forget all his retributions.

> Bless, O my soul,
> boldly the Lord;
> nor wilt thou forgetful
> ever become
> of all the goods,
> which he ere did thee.

Who is become propitious to all thy iniquities; who heals all thy sicknesses.

> He to thy evil deeds
> all has shown mercy
> and thy ailings
> all has healed.

Who has redeemed thy life from destruction; who fills in good things thy desire.

> Who redeemed thy dear life
> from destruction;
> [and] filled thy will
> fairly with good.

Who crowns thee in compassion and mercy; thy youth, as the eagle's, shall be renewed.

> He has made thee victorious
> with true mercy;
> and thee with merciful
> mind confirmed:
> thou art renewed,
> to the eagle likest,
> in youth already
> become prudent.

I confess to the Lord God.

He þinum mán-dædum
miltsade eallum ;
and þine adle
ealle gehælde.

Qui redemit de interitu uitam tuam;
qui replet in bonis desiderium tuum.

Se alysde þin lif
leof of forwyrde ;
fylde þinne willan
fægere mid gode.

Qui coronat te in miseratione et misericordia; renovabitur sicut aquile iuuentus tua.

He ðe gesigefæste
soðre mildse ;
and ðe mildheorte
mode getrymede :
eart ðu edniwe
earne gelicost,
on geoguðe nu
gleaw geworden.

Confiteor Domino Deo.

Converte nos Deus salutaris noster;
et auerte iram tuam a nobis.

> Gehweorf us hraðe,
> hælend Drihten;
> and ðin yrre fram us
> eac oncyrre.

Dignare Domine die isto sine peccato nos custodire*.

> Mildsa us nu þa,
> mihtig Drihten,
> mildsa us.

Fiat misericordia tua super nos, quemadmodum speravimus in te.

> Wese þin mildheortnis,
> mihtig Drihten,
> well ofer us,
> swa we wenað on þe.

Domine saluum fac regem; et exaudi nos in die qua inuocauerimus te.

* The Saxon of this and Latin of next omitted,—

Turn us, God our Saviour; and turn away thy wrath from us.

> Turn us quickly,
> saviour Lord;
> and thy anger from us
> also avert.

Deign, Lord, this day to guard us without sin.

> Have mercy on us now,
> mighty Lord,
> have mercy on us.

Let thy mercy be upon us, as we have hoped in thee.

> Be thy mercy,
> mighty Lord,
> well over us,
> as we hope in thee.

Lord, make safe the king; and hear us in the day in which we call upon thee.

[Miserere nostri, Domine, miserere nostri.]

>   Make, O Lord, the king
>   by deeds safe ;
>   and us also hear
>   with gracious mood,
>   on such [of] days as we
>   call to thee, Lord.

Save thy people, Lord ; and bless thy heritage ; and rule them and exalt them to eternity.

>   Heal thy people,
>   holy Lord ;
>   and all thy heritage
>   also bless ;
>   govern thou them also,
>   that they to [all] ages
>   in joys may live.

Peace be in thy strength, and abundance in thy towers.

>   Be to thee in thy strong-hold peace
>   most and foremost* ;
>   and in thy towers be
>   for the times abundance.

>   * Properly foremest, *i. e.* form-est.

Do, Drihten, cyng
dædum halne;
and us eac gehyr
holdum mode,
swilce we ðe daga,
Drihten, cigen.

Saluum fac populum tuum Domine; et benedic hereditati tue; et rege eos et extolle illos in æternum.

Hal do þin folc,
halig Drihten;
and ðin yrfe eac
eall gebletsa;
rece þu heo swylce,
þæt hi on worulde
wynnum* lifigen.

Fiat pax in uirtute tua; et abundantia in turribus tuis.

Sy þe on ðinum mægne sib
mæst and fyrmest;
and on þinum torrum wese
tidum genihtsum.

* MS. ꞃýnnum.—"Peaceably." Hickes.

Domine, exaudi orationem meam; et clamor meus ad te perueniat.

>Đu min gebed,
>mære Drihten,
>gehyr, heofones Weard;
>and gehlyde min
>to ðe becume,
>þeoda Reccend.

Miserere mei Deus secundum magnam misericordiam tuam.

>Mildsa me, mihtig Drihten,
>swa ðu manegum dydest,
>æfter ðinre þære mycelan
>mildheortnysse.

Domine Deus uirtutum conuerte nos; et ostende faciem tuam, et salui erimus.

>Gehweorf us, mægna God,
>and us milde æteow
>þinne andwlitan,
>ealle we beoð hale.

Domine sancte, Pater omnipotens,

Lord, hear my prayer; and let my cry come to thee.

> Hear thou my prayer,
> glorious Lord,
> heaven's Guardian;
> and let my shouting
> come to thee,
> Ruler of peoples.

Pity me, O God, according to thy great mercy.

> Have mercy on me, mighty Lord,
> as thou to many hast done
> after thy great
> mercy.

Lord God of virtues, convert us, and shew thy face, and we shall be safe.

> Turn us, God of mights,
> and to us mildly shew
> thy countenance,
> all we shall be whole.

Holy Lord, almighty Father, eternal

God, who hast made us to come to the beginning of this day, save us by thy power, that in this day we may decline to no sin, but always our words may proceed, and our works be directed to do thy righteousness.

Precious in the Lord's view is the death of his saints.

May the holy mother of God, the virgin Mary, and all the saints of God, intercede for us sinners to the Lord of lords, that we may deserve to be aided and saved by him: [O Thou] who livest and reignest God, (&c.)

God, attend for my aid: Lord, hasten to help me.

> Be, Lord God,
> a precious aid;
> behold me, Lord,
> and quickly then
> assist me
> at life-need.

Glory to the Father.

æterne Deus, qui nos ad principium huius diei peruenire fecisti; tua nos salua uirtute, ut in hac die ad nullum declinemus peccatum; sed semper ad tuam iustitiam faciendam nostra procedant eloquia, et dirigantur opera.

Pretiosa est in conspectu Domini mors sanctorum eius.

Sancta Dei genetrix uirgo M ria et omnes sancti Dei intercedant pro nobis peccatoribus ad Dominum dominorum, ut mereamur ab eo adiuuari et saluari; qui uiuis et regnas Deus.

Deus in adiutorium meum intende: Domine ad adiuuandum me festina.

> Wes, Drihten God,
> deore fultum;
> beheald me, Drihten,
> and me hraðe syððan
> gefultuma
> æt feorh-þearfe.

Gloria Patri.

Kyrie eleison.
Pater noster.
Et ne nos inducas.

Respice in seruos tuos, et in opera tua Domine; et dirige filios eorum.

>Geseoh þine scealcas
>swæsum eagum,
>and on þin agen weorc,
>ece Drihten;
>and heora bearn gerece
>bliðum mode.

Et sit splendor Domini Dei nostri super nos; et opera manuum nostrarum dirige super nos.

>Wese us beorhtnys ofer
>bliðan Drihtnes ures,
>þæs godan Godes,
>georne ofer ealle;
>gerece ure hand-geweorc
>heah ofer usic.

Oremus. Dirigere et sanctificare et

Lord have pity.
Our Father.
And lead us not in- - -

Look upon thy servants, and upon thy works, Lord, and direct their sons.

> Look upon thy servants
> with pleasant eyes,
> and on thy own work,
> eternal Lord:
> and direct their children
> with a cheerful mind.

And let the brightness of the Lord our God be upon us; and the works of our hands direct thou upon us.

> Be over us the brightness
> of our kind Lord,
> the good God,
> freely over all;
> direct our hand-ywork
> high over us.

Let us pray.—Lord God, King, Creator of heaven and earth, we beseech thee to-day that thou daily deign to direct, sanctify and govern our hearts and bodies, our actions also and speeches, in thy law, and in the precepts of thy commandments; that here and everywhere we may deserve by thee to be always safe and free, O Saviour of the world, who with the Father and the Holy Ghost livest and reignest God through all ages of ages. Amen. Our aid [is] in the name of the Lord, who made heaven and earth.—Bless ye.—May God the Son of God deign to bless us. Amen.

Of the Office of the third hour.

At Undern we ought to praise God, because at undern-time Christ was by the judgement of the Jews condemned to death, and led toward the cross, on which he afterwards suffered for the redemption of the whole world. On the day of Pentecost came the Holy Ghost

regere digneris Domine Deus rex creator cœli et terræ hodie quesumus cotidie corda et corpora nostra, actus quoque et sermones nostros in lege tua, et in preceptis mandatorum tuorum; ut hic et ubique per te semper salui et liberi æsse mereamur, Saluator mundi; qui cum Patre et Spiritu Sancto uiuis et regnas Deus per omnia secula seculorum. Amen. Adiutorium nostrum in nomine Domini, qui fecit cœlum et terram. Benedicite. Deus Dei Filius nos benedicere dignetur. Amen.

De officio tertiæ horæ. (*Undern-sang.*)

On undern we sculon God herian, forðam on undern-timan Crist wæs ðurh þara Iudea dom to deaðe fordemed, and toweard þære rode gelæd, þe he syððan on þrowode for ealles middan-eardes alysednysse; and eft, æfter his æriste, on pentecostenes dæg com se Halga Gast on undern-timan ofer ða apostolas, þær hi ætgædere gesamnode wæron, and hi ealle sona gefyllede wurdon swa swyðe mid Godes gyfe, þæt hi eallra gereorda getingnesse hæfdon, and heora lar wearð geond ealne middan-eard syððan gecyðed and gedæled þeodum to helpe. Undern is dæges ðridde tid; þonne is eac rihtlic þæt we to þære þriddan tide þa halgan ðrynnesse geornlice herian.

Deus in adiutorium meum intende.
Gloria Patri.

Hymnus.

Nunc Sancte nobis Spiritus.

Psalmus.—Capitel.

Gratia uobis et pax a Deo Patre nostro et Domine Jesu Christo.

Deo Gratias.
Kyrrie leison.
Christe leison.
Cyrrie leison.
Pater noster.

at undern-time upon the Apostles, where they were assembled together; and immediately they were all filled so powerfully with God's grace, that they had the faculty of all languages; and their doctrine was afterwards made known and dispersed through all the world for a help to the nations. Undern is the third hour of the day; then it is also right that we at the third hour heartily praise the holy Trinity.

God attend to my aid.
Glory to the Father.
Hymn.
Now to us, O holy Spirit.
Psalm.—Chapter.
Grace to you and peace from God the Father and the Lord Jesus Christ.
Thanks to God.
Lord have mercy.
Christ have mercy.
Lord have mercy.
Our Father.

I said, Lord, be merciful to me; heal my soul, for I have sinned to thee.

>I now with might said,
>Be merciful to me, Lord;
>heal my soul,
>for it repents me now
>that I crimes against thee
>committed abundantly.

Turn, Lord, a little, and be exorable for thy servants.

>Turn us a little,
>holy Lord;
>be to thy servants
>very easily entreated.

Send them help, O Lord.
Lord, hear.
The Lord [be] with us.

Lord God, who at the third hour of the day, for the salvation of the world, wast led to the punishment of the cross, we humbly entreat thee, that we may always find with thee pardon of our

Ego dixi, Domine miserere mei; sana animam meam, quia peccavi tibi.

 Ic nu mægene cweþe
 miltsa me Drihten;
 hæl mine sawle,
 forðon me hreoweð nu,
 þæt ic firene on ðe
 fremed geneahhige.

Convertere, Domine, aliquantulum; et deprecabilis esto super seruos tuos.

 Gehweorf us hwæt-hwyga,
 halig Drihten;
 wes ðinum scealcum
 wel eað-bene. (-bede.)

Mitte eis Domine auxilium.
Domine exaudi.
Dominus nobiscum.

Domine Deus qui hora tertia diei ad crucis pœnam pro mundi salute ductus es, te suppliciter deprecamur. ut de preteritis malis nostris semper apud te inueniamus ueniam; et de futuris iu-

giter habeamus custodiam: qui cum Patre.

De Officio sexte horc. (*Middæg-sang.*)

On midne dæg we sculon God herian, forðam to middes dæges Crist wæs on rode aðened; and us ealle þa þurh his ðrowunge, mid his deorwyrðan blode gebohte of deofles anwealde and of ecan deaðe: and ðy we sculon on ðone timan to Criste beon georne clypigende, and hine herigende; þæt we mid þam geswytelian, þæt we gemyndige beon þære myclan mildheortnysse, þe he on mancynne geworhte, þa ða he let hine sylfne syllan to cwale for mancynnes þearfe.

Deus in adiutorium meum intende.
Gloria Patri.

Ymnus.
Rector potens uerax.

past evils, and may continually have safeguard for the future: who with the Father.

Of the Office of the sixth hour.

At mid-day we ought to praise God, because at mid-day Christ was extended on the cross; and then through his suffering bought us all with his precious blood from the devil's power and from eternal death: and therefore we ought at that time to be eagerly crying to Christ, and praising him that we may thereby manifest that we are mindful of the great mercy which he wrought on mankind, when he let give himself to torture for mankind's necessity. (*profit*.)

God to my help attend.
Glory to the Father.

HYMN.
Ruler mighty [and] true.

CHAPTERS.

But prove all things, hold that which is good: abstain [yourselves] from every evil appearance. Thanks to God. The Lord rules me. Lord have mercy. Christ have mercy. Lord have mercy.

COLLECT.

Lord Jesus Christ, who at the sixth hour didst for us ascend upon the cross, and didst rescue Adam from hell, and didst restore him into paradise, we pray thee that thou command to rescue us from all our sins, and keep us always in thy holy works: Jesus Christ who with (&c.).

Of the Office of the ninth hour.

At noon-time we ought to praise God, because at that time Christ prayed for those who injured him and afterwards gave up his spirit: and at that time ought faithful men earnestly to pray, and to remember the wonder

Capitula.

Omnia autem probate, quod bonum est tenete: ab omni specie mala abstinete uos. Deo gratias. Dominus regit me. Cyrrie leison. Christe leison. Kyrrie leison.

Collecta.

Domine Iesu Christe, qui sexta hora pro nobis in cruce ascendisti, et Adam de inferno eruisti, eumque in paradyso restituisti, te quesumus ut ab omnibus peccatis nostris eripere nos iubeas, et in operibus tuis sanctis semper custodias: Iesu Christe qui cum.

De Officio nonæ horæ. (*Non-sang.*)

ON NON-TIMAN we sculon God herian, forðam on þone timan Crist gebæd for ðam þe him deredon, and syððan his gast asende: and on ðone timan sculon geleafulle men hi georne gebiddan, and gemunan þæt wundor þæt ða

geworden wearð; þa se sylfa for man-
cyn deað geþolode, þe eallum mancynne
lifes geuðe.

Dominus in adiutorium meum.
Gloria Patri.

Ymnus.

Rerum Deus tenax uigor.

Capitula.

Alter alterius honera portate, et sic
adimplebitis legem Christi.

Deo gratias. Ab occultis meis munda
me Domine. Kyrriel. Christel. Kyrriel.

Collecta.

Domine Iesu Christe, qui hora nona
in crucis patibulo confitentem latronem
intra mænia paradysi transire iussisti;
tibi suppliciter confitentes peccata nostra deprecamur deleas; et post obitum
nostrum paradisi nobis gaudia introire

which then was done; when he himself suffered death for mankind, who to all mankind gave life.

Lord to my help.
Glory to the Father.

Hymn.

God, the firm strength of [all] things.

Chapters.

Bear one another's burthens, and so ye shall fulfill the law of Christ.

Thanks to God. From my secret [sins] cleanse me, Lord. Lord have mercy. Christ have mercy. Lord have mercy.

Collect.

Lord Jesus Christ, who at the ninth hour, on the gibbet of the cross, didst order the confessing robber to pass within the walls of paradise, humbly confessing our sins to thee we entreat thee to blot them out; and after our decease grant us to enter the joys of paradise,

O Saviour of the world: who with the Father (&c.).

At Evening.

At Even we ought to praise God: at that time man offered in the old law, and with smoke of frankincense in the temple willingly honoured the altar to the praise of God; and at even-time our Lord offered at his evening repast, and dealt to his disciples, by holy mystery, bread and wine, for his self's body, and for his own blood.

And at even-time it was that Joseph unfastened Christ's body from the cross. Then we have much need that we remember such [things] and thank God, and at that time willingly offer our prayers to our Lord; as David says: Let my prayer be directed to thee, Lord, as incense in thy sight.

Be in thy sight

concedas, Saluator mundi: qui cum Patre.

Ad Uesperum. (*Æfen-sang.*)

On æfen we sculon God herian: on ðone timan man offrode on þære ealdan æ, and mid recels-reocan on ðam temple þæt weofod georne weorðode Gode to lofe; and on æfen-timan ure Drihten offrode æt his æfen-gereorde, and dælde his discipulum, þurh halig geryne, hlaf and win, for his sylfes lichaman, and for his agen blod.

And on æfen-timan hit wæs þæt Ioseph Cristes lichaman of rode alinode. Þonne we agon myccle þearfe þæt we swylce gemunan and Gode þancian, and on þone timan ure gebedu urum Drihtne georne offrian; eal-swa Dauid cwæð: Dirigatur Domine ad te oratio mea sicut incensum in conspectu tuo.

Sy on ðinre gesihðe

> mines sylfes gebed
> full ricene gerebt,
> swa recels bið
> þonne gifre
> gleda bærnað.

Deus in adiutorium meum intende.
Gloria Patri.

Gratia Domini nostri Iesu Christi et caritas Dei et communicatio Spiritus Sancti sit semper cum omnibus uobis.

Deo gratias. R. Adiutorium nostrum in nomine Domini. V. Qui fecit cœlum et terram.

Hymnus.

O lux beata Trinitas.

V. Dirigatur Domine ad te oratio mea.

Eu^{gl}.

Misericordia Dei et sanctum nomen eius super timentes eum.

℣. Magnificat.

Kirrie leison.

my[self's] prayer
full quickly directed,
as incense is
when greedy
coals burn.

O God, attend to my help.
Glory to the Father.

The grace of our Lord Jesus Christ, and the love of God, and the communication of the Holy Spirit be always with you all.

Thanks to God. R. Our help is in the name of the Lord. V. Who made heaven and earth.

Hymn.

O blessed light, O Trinity.

V. Lord, let my prayer be directed to thee.

Gospel.

God's mercy and his holy name [be] upon them who fear him.

[My soul] magnifieth.
Lord have mercy.

Christ have mercy.
Lord have mercy.
Our Father.

And lead us not into temptation.
I have said prayers, Lord.

Collect.

Let us pray. At evening and morning and mid-day, we humbly entreat thy Majesty, that, the darkness of sins being expelled from our hearts, thou make us come to the true light, which is Christ.

Of Complene.

At Fore-night we ought to praise God ere we go to bed, and to remember that near fore-night Christ was buried in the tomb; and therein his body rested so long as his will was. Then have we therefore great need that we meditate upon that, and at that time betake ourselves to God, ere we go to bed, and

Criste leison.
Kirrie leison.
Pater noster.

Et ne nos inducas in temptationem.
Preces ego dixi, Domine.

COLLECTA.

Oremus. Uespere et mane et meridie, Maiestatem tuam suppliciter exoramus, ut expulsis de cordibus nostris peccatorum tenebris, ad ueram lucem, quæ Christus est, nos facias peruenire.

De Completorio. (*Foran-niht sang.*)

On foran-niht we sculon God herian ær we to bedde gan, and gemunan þæt Crist on byrgene neah foran-nihte bebyrged wearð; and þær his lichaman on gereste, swa lange swa his willa wæs. Þonne age we þæs micle þearfe, þæt we þæt geþencan, and us sylfe on þone timan Gode betæcan, ær we to bedde gan, and hine biddan þæt he us gedefre reste geunne, and wið deofles costnunga gescylde, swa his willa sy.

Conuerte nos Deus.—Deus in adiutorium meum.

Hymnus.

Te lucis ante terminum.
Christe, qui lux es, et die *
[Noctis tenebras detegis.]

In nocte.

Tu in nobis es Domine, et nomen sanctum tuum inuocatum super nos. Ne derelinquas nos Domine Deus noster. Deo gratias.

Custodi nos Domine ut pupillum oculi.

Kyrrie leison.
Christe leison.
Kyrrie leison.

Pater noster.—Credo in Deum Pa-

* Vulg. lux es et dies, Noctis— The true reading, confirmed by the Theodisc or Frankish gloss, *take* (dæge), not *tak* (dæg), may be seen in Grimm's

pray him that he grant us convenient rest, and shield us against the devil's temptations, so his will be.

Turn us, God.—God, to my help.

HYMN.

Thee before the term of light.

Christ, who art the light, and with day [unveilest the darkness of night.]

IN THE NIGHT.

Thou art in us, Lord, and thy holy name invoked over us. Forsake us not, Lord our God. Thanks to God.

Guard us, Lord, as the apple of the eye.

Lord have mercy.
Christ have mercy.
Lord have mercy.

Our Father.—I believe in God the

Hymnorum veteris ecclesiæ xxvi. Interpretatio Theotisca nunc primum edita. Götting. 1830.

Father.—Let us bless the Father.—Blessed art thou, Lord.—May almighty God bless and keep us. Amen. Deign, Lord, this night. Let us pray. Visit, Lord, this habitation, and repel far from it all the snares of the enemy: may thy angels guard us in that peace; and let thy blessing be upon us through the same [Jesus Christ.] The Lord [be] with you. Let us bless the Lord. The blessing of God the Father almighty, and of the Son, and of the Holy Ghost, remain always with you. Amen.

Of the Nocturnal Celebration.

At midnight we ought to praise God; as David says: Media nocte surgebam ad confitendum tibi super judicia justitiæ tuæ; that is, At midnight I arose, O Lord, to confess to thee concerning the judgements of thy righteousness. Christ himself commanded that we should eagerly watch: Vigilate ergo,

trem.—Benedicamus Patrem.—Benedictus es Domine.—Benedicat et custodiat nos omnipotens Deus. Amen. Dignare Domine nocte ista. Oremus. Uisita Domine habitationem istam; et omnes insidias inimici ab ea longe repelle: angeli tui nos in ea pace custodiant; et benedictio tua sit super nos per eundem. Dominus uobiscum. Benedicamus Domino. Benedictio Dei Patris omnipotentis, et Filii, et Spiritus Sancti, maneat semper uobiscum. Amen.

De Nocturna Celebratione. (Uht-sang.)

On uhtan we sculon God herian; eal-swa Dauid cwæð: Media nocte surgebam ad confitendum tibi super iudicia iustitiæ tuæ; ðæt is, To middre nihte ic aras Drihten, et cetera. Crist sylf bead þæt we georne wacian sceoldan; he cwæð: Uigilate ergo quia nescitis

quando ueniet Dominus; þæt bið:
Waciað georne; forðam þe ge nyton
hwænne eower Drihten cymð. And
eft he cwæð: Beati serui illi quos cum
uenerit Dominus; þæt is, Eadige beoð
þa men þe se Hlaford wacigende gemet,
þonne he tocymð. Us is mycel ðearf
þæt we geornlice wacian and wære beon;
forþam nele deað na cyðan hwænne he
cuman wyle, þe ma þe þeof; ac he cymþ
þonne man læst wenð. Þonne bið se
swyðe gesælig se þe bið þonne wacigende:
Se bið wacigende ðe asmeað
ymbe Godes willan and ymbe his agene
þearfe, and on ðam geendað: And se
bið sleac and slæpende, se þe fullgæð
eallum his lyðrum lustum þurh deofles
lare, and on ðam geendað.

And þonne age we mycle þearfe, þæt
we geornlice wacian, and á wære beon
wið deofles costnunga, and þæt we georne
to Gode clypian, and æt him ge-

quia nescitis quando veniet Dominus; that is, Watch eagerly; for ye know not when your Lord shall come. And again he says: Beati servi illi quos cum venerit Dominus; that is, Blessed shall be those men whom the Lord shall find watching, when he comes. We have great need that we eagerly watch and beware; for death will not shew when he will come, more than a thief; but he comes when man least expects. Then shall he be very happy, who shall then be watching: He is watching who meditates about God's will, and about his own necessities, and in them ends [his life]. And he is slothful and sleeping, who, through the devil's instigation, accomplishes all his wicked desires, and in them ends.

And therefore have we great need, that we eagerly watch, and ever beware against the devil's temptations; and that we heartily cry to God, and obtain from him that he assist us by his mercy; that we at our ending-time may be so watching in good deeds, that we ever afterwards may rest us in eternal rest.

Now I have in some part touched concerning the daily hour-offices, which man ought to perform as necessary duty.

Then there is much need that man understand that man in addition to that, shall often and unseldom praise God, and cry to God for many needs; as the apostle says: Sine intermissione orate; that is, Be aye incessantly praying. And again the apostle says: Sive enim manducatis sive bibitis, sive aliud quid facitis, omnia in gloriam Dei facite; that is, If ye eat or drink or elsewhat work, whatsoever ye do*, do all thanking and praising God. Be the thing what it may be, that the man will work to profit, let him pray God for

* Or, do what you may.

earnian, þæt he us gefylste þurh his mildheortnysse; þæt we on urum endetiman swa wacigende beon on gódum dædum, þæt we syððan á us gerestan magan and motan on ecere reste.

Nu ic hæbbe be suman dæle ahrepod be ðam dæghwamlican tid-þenungum, ðe man to nydrihte don sceall.

Ðonne is mycel þearf þæt man understande þæt man to-eacan þam oft and unseldan sceall God herian, and to Gode clypian for manegum neodan; eall-swa se apostol cwæð: Sine intermissione orate; þæt is, Beoð á symble eow gebiddende. And eft se apostol cwæð: Siue enim manducatis, siue bibitis, siue aliquid qui facitis, omnia in gloriam Dei facite; þæt is, Gyf ge etan, oððon drincan, oððon elles hwæt wyrcean, don þæt ge don, doð ealle Gode þanciende and herigende. Beo þæt ðinga þæt hit beo þæt se man to note wyrcean wylle, bidde he God fultumes:

á á him spewð þe bet; eall-swa Dauid cwæð: Adiutor meus esto Domine; þæt is, Min Drihten, beo min fultum. And eft he cwæð: Adiutorium nostrum in nomine Domini, qui fecit celum et terram.

>Ure fultum is* God,
>þe gesceop and geworhte
>heofonas and eorðan,
>and ealle gesceafta:
>God us gefultumige
>to ure ðearfe,
>swa his wylla sy.
>Amen.

* On Drihtnes naman gelang. Cod. MS. S. 18. C. C. C. C. ap. Wanley.

P. 198, R. *for* Responsum. V.—Vesper?

aid: ever and aye he will speed the better; as David says: Adjutor meus esto Domine; that is, My Lord, be my help. And again he says: Adjutorium nostrum in nomine Domini, qui fecit cœlum et terram.

> Our help is God,
> who shaped and wrought
> heavens and earth,
> and all creatures:
> God assist us
> at our need,
> so his will be.
> Amen.

P. 206, *last*, æt—to, *MS.* P. 209, 7. tidan þenungan, *MS.*

The monastic spelling in michi, æsse, kyrrieleison, &c. *pleads MS. authority.*

PRAYERS IN SAXON.

I.

O dear Lord,
O good Judge,
spare me,
eternal Potentate,
I know my soul
wounded by sins;
heal thou her,
Lord of heavens;
and cure thou her,
Prince of life;
for thou most easily canst
of all physicians
that have been
far or wide.

II.

O bright Lord,
Creator of people,
mitigate thy mind

PRECATIONES SAXONICE.

Bibliothec. Cott. Jul. A. II.

Æla Drihten leóf,
æla Dema gód,
ge-ára me,
éce Waldend.
Ic wat mine saule
synnum forwundod;
gehæl ðu hy,
heofena Drihten;
and gelacna ðu hy,
lifes Ealdor;
forþan ðu eðest miht
ealra læca,
þæra þe gewurde
side oððe wide.

Æla Frea beorhta,
folkes Scippend,
gemilsa þyn mod

me to gode;
sile þyne are,
þyne earminge.
Se byð earming,
þe on eorðan her
dæiges and nihtes
deoflon campað,
and his willan wyrcð:
wa him þære mirigðe,
þonne he þa handlean
hafað and sceawað,
bute he þæs yfeles
ær geswice.
Se byð eadig,
se þe on eorðan her
dæiges and nyhtes
Drihtne hyræð,
and á hys willan wyrcð.
wel hym þæs geweorkes,
þonne he ða handlean
hafað and sceawað,
gyf he ealteawne
ende gedreogeð.

for good to me;
grant thy mercy,
thy commiseration.
He is miserable,
who on earth here
day and night
fights for the devil,
and works his will;
woe to him of the mirth,
when he the reward
has and sees,
unless he from the evil
previously depart.
He is happy,
who on earth here
day and night
obeys the Lord
and aye his will works ·
weal to him of the working,
when he the reward
has and sees,
if he a good
end shall make.

III.

O Light of lights,
O joy of life,
bestow on me,
most glorious King,
(when I for my soul
ask heaven,)
eternal mercy.
Thou art clearly God,
hast and rulest,
alone over all,
of earth and heaven
the wide creation.
Thou art the true Creator
alone over all
earth's inhabitants,
likewise in heaven above.
Thou art the Saviour God;
thee cannot praise
any of men,
though to us we assemble
throughout the ample ground
men above the mould
through all the mid-region,

Æla leohtes leoht,
æla lifes wynn,
getiþa me,
tir-eadig Kyning,
þonne ic minre sawle
swegles bydde,
ece are.
Ðu eart eaðe God,
hæfst and waldest,
ana ofer ealle,
eorðan and heofonas
syddra gesceafta.
Ðu eart soð Meotod
ana ofer ealle
eorð-bugende,
swilce on heofonum up.
Ðu eart Hælend God;
ne mæg ðe aherian
hæleða ænig;
þeh us gesomnie
geond sidne grund
men ofer moldan
geond ealne middan-eard,

ne mæge we næfre asæcgan,
ne þæt soð witan,
hu ðu æðele eart,
ece Drihten;
ne þeah engla werod
up on heofonum
snotra tosomne
sæcgan ongunnon,
ne magon hy næfre areccean,
ne þæt gerim wytan,
hu ðu mære eart,
mihtig Drihten;
ac is wunder mycel,
Wealdend engla,
gif ðu hit sylfa wast,
sigores Ealdor,
hu ðu mære eart*,
mihtig and mægen-strang,
ealra kyninga Kyning,
Crist lifiend,
ealra worulda Scippend,
Wealdend engla,

* This thought appears to be original, and be-
wrays, as we may say, an effort to solve the tran-

never can we express,
nor the truth know,
how noble thou art,
eternal Lord;
nor though the host
up in heaven
of skilful angels together
should begin to say,
they never can declare,
nor the number know,
how glorious thou art,
mighty Lord;
but there is much wonder,
Governor of angels,
if thou thyself knowest,
Prince of triumph,
how glorious thou art,
mighty and main-strong,
of all kings King,
living Christ,
Creator of all worlds,
Governor of angels,

scendental problem—Can the Infinite comprehend the Infinite?

Virtue of all virtues,
Lord Jesus.
Thou art the Noble,
whom in former days
the Joy of all virgins
gloriously brought forth
in the city Bethlehem
for a comfort to men,
for mercy to all
the children of time,
who believe
in the living God,
and in the eternal light,
up in the skies.
Thy power is so majestic,
mighty Lord,
that any one
of earth's inhabitants
knows not the depth
of the Lord's might;
and that any one
of the order of angels
knows not the height
of heaven's King.

ealra dugeþa duguð,
Drihten Hælend.
Ðu eart se Æþela,
ðe on ær-dagum
ealra fæmnena wyn
fægere akende
on Bethleem þære byrig,
beornum to frofre,
eallum to are
ylda bearnum,
þam ðe gelyfað
on lyfiendne God,
and on þæt ece leoht
uppe on roderum.
Ðyn mægen is swa mære,
mihtig Drihten,
swa þæt ænig ne wat
eorð-buenda (-de, *MS.*)
þa deopnesse
Drihtnes mihta;
ne þæt ænig ne wat
engla hades
þa heahnisse
heofena Kyninges.

Ic ðe andette,
ælmihtig God,
þæt ic gelyfe on ðe,
leofa Hælend,
þæt ðu eart se miccla,
and se mægen-stranga,
and se eadmoda
ealra goda,
and se ece Kyning
ealra gesceafta;
and ic eom se litla for þe,
and se lyðra man,
se her syngige
swiðe genehhe,
dæges and nihtes,
do swa ic ne sceolde,
hwile mid weorce,
hwile mid worde,
hwile mid geþohte,
þearle scildi,
inwit-niðas
oft and gelome.
Ac ic ðe halsige nu,
heofena Drihten,

I confess to thee,
almighty God,
that I believe on thee,
dear Saviour,
that thou art the great,
and the strong in might,
and the lowly
of all gods,
and the eternal King
of all creatures ;
and I am the little, before thee,
and the wicked man,
who here sin
very abundantly,
day and night,
do as I should not
(sometimes with work,
sometimes with word,
sometimes with thought,
horribly guilty,)
heinous offences
oft and frequently.
But I beseech thee now,
Lord of heavens,

and pray to thee,
best of princes*,
that thou have mercy on me,
mighty Lord,
high King of heavens,
and the holy Ghost;
and assist me,
Father almighty,
that I thy will
may perform,
ere I from this meagre
life depart.
Refuse not thou me,
Lord of glory;
but grant me,
most glorious King;
let me with angels
mount aloft,
sit in the sky,
praise heaven's God
with holy speech
ages without end.
Amen.

* Or of men, heroes, warriors.

and gebidde me to þe,
beorna* selost,
þæt ðu gemilsige me,
mihtig Drihten,
heofena Heah-kyning,
and se halga Gast;
and gefylste me,
Fæder ælmihtig,
þæt ic þinne willan
gewyrcean mæge,
ær ic of ðysum hiænan
lyfe gehweorfe.
Ne forweorn þu me,
wuldres Drihten;
ac getyþa me,
tyr-eadig Kyning:
læt me mid englum
up-siðian,
sittan on swegle,
herian heofonas God
haligum reorde
á buton ende.
Amen.

* Bearna, MS.—" æðelust beorna.' Elene.

Additional Notes.

In the translation, to avoid inversion, the Saxon (and German) "man," equivalent to Fr. "on," i. e. *hom* for *homme*, has occasionally been employed as modern English.

In the last hymn, the genitive or possessive case of heofon occurs twice in a form not recognised by grammarians—heofonas; and as it is found in other places also, in MSS. of the best quality, I have not scrupled to let it appear in print. The reader is left to his choice, whether he shall make it heofones or heofona; or consider it better as it is. For who can deny that it may be a more ancient form than heofones?—Compare Runic Hifunæs, and Old [continental] Saxon gen. in *as* or *es*.

Perhaps the translation p. 216, 9, 11, should be "rulest . . . , earth and heaven," &c. —still, wealdest governs the genitive.

The epithet ealra fæmnena wyn, p. 221, might be rendered "Queen of all virgins;" as another poet's Lagu-floda wyn may find an equivalent in "King of floods."—Thomson's Seasons.

NOTE.

The Illustrations of this Volume are derived from materials of the Anglo-Saxon period.

The Frontispiece, representing the Crucifixion, has been very carefully traced (by special permission of the Trustees of the British Museum) from the Cottonian Manuscript, Titus D. 27, executed at Hyde Abbey, A. D. 976. In the original the outlines of the flesh and of portions of the dresses are in red, the remainder being drawn in black ink with a pen, with great spirit. The inscription consists of two verses :—

"Hec crux consignet Ælfpinum corpore mente,
In quam suspendens traxit Deus omnia Secum.

The label on the head of the Saviour is inscribed :—

"Hic e(st) IHS Nazerenus rex judeor(um)."

The facsimile of the Lord's Prayer is copied from the Royal MS. 7, cxii. in the British

Museum, fol. 87 a, and may also be referred to the 10th century. The version is identical with that printed in page 84 of the present volume, although some of the words are spelled differently. The Ornaments of the Binding are copied from the Missal of Bishop Leofric, in the Bodleian Library, and an Anglo-Hibernian Psalter of the ninth century, in the British Museum.

The Divine Hand, emitting triple rays of light, is from the singular Copper Font in the Church of St. Bartholomew, at Liege.

THE END.

BILLING AND SONS, PRINTERS, GUILDFORD.

www.ingramcontent.com/pod-product-compliance
Lightning Source LLC
Chambersburg PA
CBHW032059220426
43664CB00008B/1067